Underground Codes

Race, Crime, and Related Fires

Katheryn Russell-Brown

NEW YORK UNIVERSITY PRESS

New York and London

NEW YORK UNIVERSITY PRESS
New York and London
www.nyupress.org

Library of Congress Cataloging-in Publication Data
Russell-Brown, Katheryn, 1961–
Underground codes : race, crime, and related fires / Katheryn Russell-Brown.
p. cm.
Includes bibliographical references and index.
ISBN 0–8147–7540–3 (cloth : alk. paper)
ISBN 0–8147–7541–1 (pbk : alk. paper)
1. Discrimination in criminal justice administration—United States.
2. Discrimination in law enforcement—United States.
3. Crime and race—United States.   4. Minorities—United States.
I. Title.
HV9950.R873   2003
364'.08'0973—dc22   2003017314

New York University Press books are printed on acid-free paper, and
their binding materials are chosen for strength and durability.

Manufactured in the United States of America

10 9 8 7 6 5 4 3 2 1

To my husband-love,
        Kevin Kimble Brown

Contents

Acknowledgments

First, thank you to New York University Press for its continued interest in my work. As well, I thank my colleagues who read and discussed manuscript chapters with me: Sandra Bass, Angela Jordan Davis, David Harris, Darnell Hawkins, Dragan Milovanovic, Jill Nelson, Becky Tatum, Ronald Walters, and Geoffrey Ward. As well, in spring 2001, I received wonderful feedback on an early draft of the chapter on Black protectionism from participants in Princeton's African American Studies Program's Lecture Series (Works-in-Progress), headed by Noliwe Rooks. I am very appreciative of the support I received from the University of Maryland, particularly my colleagues Charles F. Wellford, John Laub, Sally Simpson, Gary LaFree, and the former dean Irwin Goldstein.

I received exceptional research assistance from several graduate students, including Greg J. Jones, Samantha Kwan, Patrice White, and undergraduate Sabastian Niles. An extra-special thank you to a former graduate student, Melissa Bamba, who managed to read and provide a detailed critique of the full manuscript in record time.

Last, I could not have completed this project without the love and support of my beloved family and dear friends.

Introduction

In the children's game of "telephone," a group of children sit in a circle and one child begins by whispering a statement or phrase into the ear of the child sitting next to her. This child then repeats the message, passing it along to the next child. This continues until the statement or phrase makes its way back around the circle. When the last person receives the message, he announces what he has heard. Typically, the statement or phrase varies so greatly from the initial one that it evokes humor and surprise. In some ways, this process—the game of telephone—is analogous to the state of affairs regarding data, perceptions, and information about race and crime.

Both the public discussion and the empirical research indicate that there are many issues involving crime and race that are overlooked, misunderstood, and falsely linked. The title of this book, *Underground Codes,* highlights this fact. As well, the title alludes to Harriet Tubman's Underground Railroad which led hundreds of slaves to freedom. Thus, a modest objective of this book is to promote a kind of "freedom" in the form of new thinking about the actual and perceived nexus between crime and race.

Since I wrote *The Color of Crime,* the national spotlight on race and crime has dimmed. The introspection demanded by larger-than-life criminal cases, such as those involving Rodney King and O. J. Simpson, is no longer a national objective. In the past few years, spectacular, racially tinged criminal cases, which pushed discomforting and vexing questions to the fore, have been replaced by larger national issues. As the psychologist Abraham Maslow's hierarchy of needs would predict, issues of national and personal security—physical and financial—took precedence over sociological inquiries. Specifically, the September 11, 2001, attacks on the United States, the collapse of several major business corporations and their accounting fallouts (e.g., Enron, WorldCom, Xerox), and the U.S. war in Iraq have altered the nation's economic, political, and social interests.

Underground Codes, however, argues that we must continue our analysis of the connection between crime and race and reconsider how this relationship is fostered, explicitly and tacitly. The text's three central goals are interrelated: (1) to outline the operating mechanisms of the criminal justice system that hamper our efforts to detect the impact of race; (2) to highlight commonly held linkages between race and crime that have little or no empirical foundation; and (3) to address important but rarely discussed issues of race and crime. Specifically, each chapter ties directly to the goal of highlighting areas of crime and race that are worthy of greater empirical attention or of analyzing ways in which crime and race are covertly linked.

The first chapter offers an example of how doing business as usual—which, in this context, means using mainstream methods to conduct research on race discrimination—perpetuates the age-old link between race and crime. This opening chapter critiques the standard methods used to assess racial discrimination in the criminal justice system. It is argued that the widely accepted analyses of racial bias obscure evidence of racial discrimination. The chapter explores the difference between the role race plays in formal stages (where official data are available) and in informal stages (where official data are not available). The findings indicate that we should expand the definition of formal stage to include other phases of the justice system, such as pre-arrest and parole. As well, this chapter provides an introduction to the issues addressed in subsequent chapters.

Chapter 2 examines how American Indians are funneled through the U.S. justice system. Most interesting, the data indicate that Indians, who constitute less than 1 percent of the U.S. population, have exceedingly high victimization rates. Between 1992 and 1996, their rates were higher than those of any other racial group, including African Americans. The chapter includes a discussion of the complex web of justice systems through which American Indians are processed, a further complication when attempting to identify and understand their crime and victimization rates. The chapter makes a case for focusing more attention on American Indians and the justice system.

Chapter 3 explores the relationship between gangsta rap music and criminal behavior. The chapter focuses on the public and legislative responses to gangsta rap music, particularly attempts to brand it as "cultural trash." A review of the empirical literature, however, reveals no direct link between listening to gangsta rap music and engaging in criminal activity.

Chapter 4 considers how police abuse and brutality are framed for public discussion. The chapter argues that, for many people, issues of police abuse and brutality are dismissed as "a Black thing" and asks where the White victims of police brutality are? It concludes with a look at the police brutality "dance"—the public, political, and legal responses to well-known abuse cases—and suggests that, absent an intervention, this process can only repeat itself.

What is the Black community's response when allegations, criminal or otherwise, are made against a Black leader or celebrity? Chapter 5 considers why, as a general rule, the Black community rallies around its fallen leaders. Further, it outlines the operating mechanisms of protectionism and identifies cases where it has been applied. The chapter considers the historical and theoretical roots of Black protectionism and critiques its application, its benefits, and its costs.

Chapter 6 focuses on racial profiling. Here, detailed attention is given to a topic that has generated national debate. The discussion includes a consideration of how profiling is defined, offers numerous examples of "Living while Black" profiling, and discusses several collateral outcomes of profiling by race.

Chapter 7 focuses on a largely overlooked race and gender group within the criminal justice system: Black women. Though African American women are the group with the fastest-growing justice system control rates, they largely remain in the shadow of African American men. This chapter offers a detailed look at the levels of involvement of Black women in the justice system, as offenders and victims, and at the reasons why their growing rates should sound loud alarm bells.

The final chapter lists twenty important race and crime facts. This list, however, is not exhaustive. The goal is to provide the reader with some foundational facts on crime and race in summary form. The list includes citations for future reference.

With each successive chapter, it becomes increasingly clear that we need a new set of lenses through which to analyze issues of race and crime. These lenses must include both wide-angle and zoom features. Developing appropriate policy responses necessitates a thorough analysis of

race and crime, an analysis that represents the next generation of thinking about crime and race.

In sum, the game of telephone sets the agenda for *Underground Codes*.
The objective of the ensuing text on race and crime is to provide a
straightforward, detailed, and illuminating discussion so that the ensuing
dialogue is an informed and ultimately productive one.

1

"Petit Apartheid" in the Justice System

I. Introduction

For decades, sociologists and criminologists have sought to explain the ceiling-high arrest, conviction, and incarceration rates of African Americans. Whether these disproportionately high rates can be reconciled by Black offense rates, racial bias, or a combination of both is subject to debate. Academic conclusions as to the presence and degree of racial bias have varied over several "waves" of research on racial disparity.[1] At the dawn of the twenty-first century, however, social scientists still had not reached accord on the impact of racial bias within the criminal justice system. On the one side, there are researchers who argue that the evidence of overall bias in the justice system is inconclusive.[2] On the other side, there are researchers who conclude that there is clear proof of race-based processing.[3] For the most part, these two camps, mainstream and alternative, respectively, employ different methods for measuring racial bias.[4] Those in the former camp rely on standard measures for evaluating the role of race. Those in the latter camp argue that the standard measures capture only observable, overt racial bias—a fraction of the overall bias within the justice system.

Daniel Georges-Abeyie, whose research falls into the second group, observes that mainstream measures of racial bias begin with arrest.[5] He notes, however, that there are numerous opportunities for racial bias to occur prior to arrest. One example is the point at which an officer decides whether to make a traffic stop. Unmeasured stages, Georges-Abeyie argues, may have causal consequences, determining, for instance, who enters the justice system. He uses the term "petit apartheid" to describe race-influenced practices in the justice system, those that are not incorporated into mainstream analyses of racial bias. In addition to pre-arrest (e.g., racially targeted stops and searches), petit apartheid encompasses trial court processes (e.g., biased judges' instructions).[6]

The goal of this chapter is to detail Georges-Abeyie's argument, which, to date, has received scant research attention.[7] The discussion has three objectives: first, to highlight the limitations of current measures of racial discrimination; second, to place petit apartheid within a theoretical framework that provides a context for understanding issues addressed in later chapters; and, third, to outline a typology that identifies the sites for racial bias within the justice system that have been overlooked by mainstream measures of racial bias. The discussion concludes that mainstream measures of racial bias function as an underground code, sending the message that crime is justifiably linked to race, Blackness in particular.

II. *Choosing a Yardstick*

As noted, the mainstream and alternative approaches to racial bias vary greatly. More detail on these differences is appropriate and necessary before there is a discussion of whether there is theoretical support for the alternative approach. The mainstream perspective views the criminal justice system as a series of discrete, observable stages, referred to as "formal" stages. As a general rule, the mainstream continuum begins with the arrest stage and ends with the sentencing stage (intervening stages include prosecutor's charge, setting of bail, jury selection, and conviction). Mainstream research on racial bias evaluates one or more of the stages between arrest and conviction; for example, whether race affects the probability of conviction or whether Blacks are more likely to be found guilty of a felony offense than similarly situated Whites.

Formal stages, the hallmark of the mainstream approach, are those that are subject to official recordkeeping. For example, each year, the FBI's Uniform Crime Reports presents data on annual arrests. As well, at the federal and state level, data are maintained in criminal cases (e.g., criminal charge, race of defendant/race of victim, type of counsel, conviction, type of sentence, and sentence length).

Mainstream studies are commonly divided into two categories; single- and multistage. Empirical evaluations that examine the effect of race at one point in the process, such as sentencing, are known as single-stage studies. All others, such as those that focus on two or more points, such as sentencing and conviction, are known as multistage studies.

In contrast to academic approaches, alternative assessments incorporate informal stages into their analyses of racial disparity and bias. Thus, an assessment of race effects is not confined to particular stages or research methods. For example, the alternative continuum begins with the first contact an individual has with an agent of the justice system, pre-arrest. It continues through the person's final contact with the justice system (e.g., parole).

The mainstream approach to racial bias raises several issues. First, most studies are limited to analyses of select stages within the justice system. They can address only whether race affects a particular stage (or stages). By design, then, they cannot determine whether race influences other stages of the process (formal or informal) or whether race has an overall affect on justice system outcomes. Although these studies may not have been designed specifically to address whether the overall justice system operates in a racially discriminatory manner, in toto, their findings have been used to support the conclusion that race does not substantively affect justice system outcomes.

Second, within mainstream analyses, "race" typically refers to the race of the offender or victim. Though the race of the victim and the defendant are important variables to study, a more diverse consideration of race may be valuable. For example, an examination of how the race of other actors within the justice system—for example, police officers, judges, attorneys, and jurors—influences decision making. Another example is to look at the interaction between the races of the various justice system officials, for instance, to look at how White offenders and Black offenders fare with Black judges compared with how each fares with White judges. The same racial analysis could be done with defense attorneys and prosecutors.

Third, mainstream research on racial disparity is heavily weighted toward case outcomes, not toward decision-making processes. Existing studies, which are mostly quantitative, focus on decision points for which statistical data are readily available for analysis (e.g., arrest). Other research methods, such as qualitative analyses, however, are also possible. Specific examples include field observations (e.g., courtroom hearings), participant observations, and interviews. Darlene Conley argues that a range of research methods is necessary to understand the impact and range of racial bias. Here she critiques the methods used to measure racial disproportionality in juvenile justice:

> Quantitative analysis dictates that the social reality of . . . youths and their communities be reduced to a few variables, such as the instant offense, arrest rates [and] violent crime rates. . . . Unfortunately, by reducing these phenomena to single indicators, the richness of the social phenomena that [researchers] are attempting to describe is lost.

Mainstream analyses typically overlook those aspects of the justice system that are not easily measured or for which comprehensive data are difficult to obtain. Therefore, as designed, these studies cannot detect the overall affect of race on judicial outcomes (e.g., sentencing).[8] Examples of overlooked analyses include whether race influences the choice of jury instructions or whether racially charged courtroom language affects case outcomes.[9]

All told, mainstream studies may offer nuanced analyses of how race affects specific aspects of the justice system. However, they are unable to provide a comprehensive picture of how racial bias influences criminal justice decision making.[10] Arguably, mainstream studies and their applications are based upon flawed models of how discrimination operates. These studies evaluate the impact of race on the formal stages of the justice system as a measure for determining whether racial discrimination permeates the whole system.

These methods appear centered around civil rights–era concerns that focus on overt racial discrimination by police and the courts. Three premises underlie this civil rights model for measuring race discrimination: first, that racial discrimination must be intentional; second, that the use of traditional indicators renders the presence or absence of racial discrimination within the justice system readily apparent and clearly identifiable; third, that racial discrimination is a discrete, insular event, and that racially biased decisions can be captured by observing particular points along the criminal justice system continuum. Thus, this approach makes it difficult to consider and evaluate the existence of systemic racial bias.

The above discussion indicates that using the term "formal" to describe select stages of the justice system process may give these stages an unwarranted legitimacy as measures for racial discrimination. In fact, there exists no intrinsic empirical distinction between those stages that have been labeled formal and those that have been labeled informal. Using the term "informal" to describe some stages may downplay their significance. In an assessment of the affect of race on justice system processing, the informal stages are arguably as important as the so-called formal stages. In view of this, hereafter, the terms "measured" and "unmeasured" stages are preferred over "formal" and "informal" stages. All told, a thorough analysis of how race affects the justice system requires a broader evaluation, one that captures both superficial and recessed processes. The following section sketches the theoretical framework for understanding the role and impact of various stages of the justice system. Specifically, it unmasks the underground coding of race and its justice system outcomes.

III. Theoretical Overview:
Placing Petit Apartheid under a Sociolegal Umbrella

This section attempts to construct a theoretical scaffold for investigating petit apartheid. This is accomplished by offering an overview of some sociological and legal theories that consider how informal and hidden processes within the justice system affect case outcomes. Each of the four perspectives discussed below provides context for understanding how disparate racial treatment is manifested within the justice system.

Georges-Abeyie is not the first researcher to consider the importance of evaluating the unmeasured or hidden stages of social institutions. In *The Presentation of Self in Everyday Life*, the sociologist Erving Goffman discusses the "back region," also referred to as the "back stage." He defines this as a place, "relative to a given performance, where the impression fostered by the performance is knowingly contradicted as a matter of course."[11] What appears in the front region is presumed to be a statement of reality—the way things are. In fact, however, the front and back regions are inextricably linked; one informs the other. Goffman labels this "impression management."[12] His analysis is valuable because it effectively demonstrates that what goes on away from the public gaze is as important as what takes place within public view. Further, those who control the back stage may have a vested interest in *not* disclosing its nature, practices, and processes.

Though Goffman applied his analysis of the back stage to individuals, it can also be applied to George-Abeyie's discussion of unmeasured stages

within the justice system. The back stage is the place where racially motivated decisions are made. Examples of the back stage include bench
conferences, jury deliberations, and police department policies that encourage racial targeting of minorities. By definition, there is little official
documentation of what occurs during these unmeasured stages. Thus, accountability is minimal. As Goffman's thesis predicts, racially motivated
decisions made in the back stage may be easily represented as racially
neutral ones in the front region. It is also noted that not all back stages
are out of view; some simply are not subject to official recordkeeping or
systematic scrutiny. An example is the use of racially charged courtroom
language by judges and attorneys. Applying Goffman's analysis to another criminal justice context, Tim Bynum and Ray Paternoster state:
"[Racial bias] . . . can more readily be conducted in hidden or backstage
regions, such as parole hearings. Past research has ignored this contextual
element, which may explain the inconsistencies in the literature."[13]

Charles Lawrence's legal analysis of unconscious racism complements
Goffman's back stage thesis. Lawrence assesses the covert, unconscious
mechanisms that allow racism to exist and proliferate in society. Even
when challenged as unconstitutional, these racialized practices often es-
cape sanction. According to Lawrence, courts are not institutionally
equipped to notice various forms of racial bias, especially those that are
subtle. This permits instances of racial bias to go unchecked and unsanc-
tioned. To remedy this blind spot, Lawrence offers the "cultural meaning" test. This test offers a measure of bias that does not require a show-
ing of overt bias or intent. The cultural meaning test could be used to assess whether a particular law or policy operates in a racially biased
manner. It would provide courts with a broader indication of how race
influences decision making: "The test would evaluate the governmental
conduct to see if it conveys a symbolic message to which the culture at-
taches racial significance."[14]

Lawrence argues that such undercover legal work is necessary because
society "no longer condones overt racist attitudes and behavior."[15] Con-
sequently, true racial attitudes surface through the "collective use of actions, words or signs [that] represent shared but repressed attitudes."[16] By
way of example, Lawrence highlights *Memphis v. Greene,* a 1981 U.S.
Supreme Court case, which challenged the construction of a wall that sep-
arated a Black community from a White community in Memphis.[17] The
lawsuit alleged that the wall was built to keep Blacks segregated from
Whites, in violation of the Fourteenth Amendment. The Court held that

because the city did not intentionally act in a racially discriminatory manner, there was no constitutional violation. Lawrence points out that if the Court had applied the cultural meaning test, it would have weighed several factors, including the amount of White flight before the wall was erected. He argues that, in evaluating the affect of race on legal and social policy, it is imperative to consider both historical and contemporary contexts.

Lawrence's analysis connects directly with Judge A. Leon Higginbotham's legal assessment of how race affects courtroom procedures. Higginbotham states that racially disparate treatment is an integral part of the "ten precepts of American slavery jurisprudence."[18] His thesis considers the affect of race, racial language, and racial incidents on the justice process. Higginbotham's critique focuses on racialized courtroom practices:

> [I]nstances of courtroom racism act as signals, triggering and mobilizing those racist attitudes and stereotypes in the minds of all the courtroom participants, and possibly affecting the judgment and actions of the judge, jury and attorneys. . . . Racist occurrences in the courts are particularly powerful symbols, acting to reinforce, legitimate, and perpetuate racism in the broader society.[19]

Higginbotham cites numerous examples of overt and covert references to race, which either reveal hidden racial biases or appear to be designed to sway legal decisionmakers. He makes several observations about the role and function of race within the justice system. First, courtroom officers are not immune from racism in society. Second, permitting the use of racial references in the courtroom to rely upon stereotypes or impact perceptions encourages other courtroom personnel to rely on racial imagery and bias (conscious or unconscious). As well, Higginbotham notes, racism in the courtroom serves a third function: It sends a message to society at large that racism is an acceptable practice. Thus, racism in court operates as a cultural symbol. Court decisions are not simply a microcosm of society but also a statement about our society.

Higginbotham's analysis is supported by the research findings of other legal scholars. For example, Sheri Johnson, after reviewing scores of criminal cases, finds a daunting array of ways that racial imagery has been used by prosecutors during their closing arguments.[20] This includes language that portrays Blackness as symbolic of evil, violence, inferiority, sexual obsession, and dishonesty. Following a detailed evaluation of the harms of unchecked racial imagery in court, Johnson concludes that existing safeguards are not adequate. What is needed, Johnson argues, is a "racial imagery shield law."[21] Such a law would prohibit the following: (1) unnecessary references to race; (2) inferences that a person's race makes him more likely to engage in crime; and (3) suggestions that a person's race makes him less worthy of credibility or respect.[22]

Randall Kennedy's examination of how the "N" word has been used in court provides additional support for Higginbotham's thesis.[23] Kennedy analyzes how the "N" word has been employed by judges, prosecutors, witnesses, and jurors. He also considers how courts have responded to charges that such language is constitutionally protected and should not be punished. Like Higginbotham, Kennedy expresses concern about the effect of racially charged language in court proceedings.

Adding yet another step in the petit apartheid theoretical chain is the work of Donald Black. In *Sociological Justice*, Black argues that the law operates as a quantitative variable.[24] He maintains that the amount of law brought to bear in a particular case (e.g., whether an arrest is made), the type of law applied (e.g., whether charges are filed), and the ultimate sanction (e.g., sentence) are variable. How the law operates in a particular instance depends upon a range of factors, including the social status of the parties, the defendant's legal representation, and his interaction with other courtroom actors (e.g., judge, witnesses, and jurors). Race is one of the factors that directly influences case processing outcomes. Ultimately, Black concludes that, across cases, the application of law is not predetermined. Rather, how the law operates is determined by "the sociology of the case."[25] The interaction between legal and extralegal variables, such as the type of case and the race, gender, and economic class of the offender and the courtroom actors, affects how cases are decided. Accordingly, Black concludes, general pronouncements about how the law operates are always false.

Together, the work of Goffman, Lawrence, Higginbotham, and Black establishes a solid foundation for Georges-Abeyie's petit apartheid thesis. Each offers a distinct and compelling rationale for looking beyond the standard measures of racial discrimination. Goffman posits that what takes place in the back region is not readily apparent to the outside world. What happens in this hidden arena, however, is directly linked to what is presented in the front arena. Further, Lawrence suggests that when legislative or political motives are not socially acceptable (e.g., racially discriminatory actions), attempts will be made to sanitize them. Racial animus that surfaces in the back stage will not voluntarily be placed in public view, the front stage. Lawrence concludes that intentional racial discrimination cannot be used as the sole test to measure the existence of racial discrimination.

Adding to Lawrence, Higginbotham illustrates how racial messages are used in the courtroom to perpetuate notions of Black inferiority. Additionally, some decisions are made outside the courtroom, away from public view. These, too, impact the justice system process. Higginbotham observes that various courtroom actors have back stages. The justice system itself is influenced by larger, society-level representations of race. In the absence of adequate checks and balances, Higginbotham argues, courts are allowed to play out racialized scripts. Black's analysis allows for an assessment of how a confluence of case-specific factors—salient among them the race of the offender—predicts that Black offenders will experience harsher treatment than Whites at each stage in the criminal justice process. The combined offerings of Goffman, Lawrence, Higginbotham, and Black illustrate how micro- and macro-level forces intersect and work to reproduce the status quo.

Petit apartheid practices have four distinct features. First, they occur largely out of public view. Second, even when they take place within plain view, they are typically minimized or ignored. Third, petit apartheid proliferates where criminal justice personnel have high levels of unchecked discretion. Fourth, these practices reflect and reinforce the racialized images of deviance that exist within society at large. The next section charts some of the locations and forms of petit apartheid.

IV. Outline of a Preliminary Typology

The broad strokes of a petit apartheid typology are outlined in table 1-1. The stages listed between the shaded areas indicate mainstream measures of racial discrimination. The shaded areas (pre-arrest and postsentence) indicate data sources that are not captured by these measures. The sketch identifies some of the legislative and policy mechanisms that enable racial bias to proliferate within the justice system (pre-arrest to postsentencing). Table 1-1 provides some indication of how much is missed by traditional evaluations of racial discrimination and disparity. First, the petit apartheid analyses both moves back the time for beginning the analysis (from arrest to pre-arrest) and extends the time for the analysis (from sentencing to postsentencing). Second, the offered typology argues for including additional places within the traditional framework for evaluating the affect of race (e.g., the use of racially charged language in the courtroom). Overall, the petit apartheid typology offers an individual, group, and institutional level calculus for racial discrimination in the justice system.

Additionally, there are broader approaches to the study of petit apartheid. For example, another model that has been offered includes nonverbal discriminatory practices that may affect the justice system. An examination of nonverbal actions would include a study of gestures, postures, and mannerisms (e.g., those indicating respect, disapproval, or interest). One way to evaluate this would be to examine the body language used by judges in their communications with defendants and witnesses.[26]

Locations and Forms of Petit Apartheid

Many race-neutral laws have had a disparate impact upon minorities (table 1-1). The antigang legislation challenged in *Chicago v. Morales* illustrates the law's impact on the pre-arrest stage of the justice system and how racial fears may be the impetus for enacting legislation in minority communities.[27] In *Morales,* the U.S. Supreme Court heard a challenge to Chicago's Gang Congregation Ordinance, under which a police officer who observed a "criminal street gang member loitering in any public place with one or more persons"[28] could require them to move along or make an arrest. As written, the law allowed police to arrest gang and nongang members. For example, a person waiting to hail a taxi or standing

TABLE 1-1
Petit Apartheid Typology

	Pre-Arrest	Arrest	Charge Decision
Legislation	• Antigang laws		• Juvenile waiver
Policies and Practices	• Racial profiling • Fetal endangerment policies		

in a doorway to avoid the rain could be stopped under the Chicago law. During the three years the law was in effect, the police issued more than eighty-nine thousand dispersal orders and made more than forty-two thousand arrests. The majority of the people charged under the ordinance were Black or Hispanic. Opponents of the law argued that it allowed for arbitrary police enforcement and violated citizens' due process rights. The Supreme Court agreed and struck down the law as unconstitutional.

Juvenile waivers offer another location for analyzing racial bias. For example, California's law, passed in 2000 (proposition 21), allows the prosecutor to charge and try juveniles age 14 or older in adult court.[29] By law, prosecutors can bypass a juvenile court "fitness" hearing and directly file charges against juvenile offenders in adult court for select offenses, including instances where a minor is accused of committing a crime in conjunction with a criminal street gang, using a firearm while committing a felony, or committing an offense that would be death-penalty-eligible if committed by an adult. As well, the law provides for an automatic judicial waiver to adult court for juveniles charged with certain types of murder or serious sex offenses. Laws permitting prosecutorial or judicial waiver exist in a handful of jurisdictions, including Florida, Pennsylvania South Carolina, and Utah.[30]

While this legislation is ostensibly race neutral, a look at how juvenile waivers are applied indicates that race influences outcomes.[31] Specifically, the research shows that, when researchers control for offense type, they find that minority youth are much more likely to be waived over to adult criminal court than White youth. This racial disparity continues through conviction and sentencing.[32] Placing the power to waive solely with prosecutors increases the probability of racial disproportionality.

TABLE 1-1 *(Continued)*
Petit Apartheid Typology

Jury Selection	Conviction	Sentence	Postsentence
		• Mandatory minimums • Two/three strikes legislation	• Parole hearings • Felony disenfranchisement
	• Closed hearings • Bench conferences • Jury deliberations • Courtroom language (e.g., opening and closing arguments)		

Beyond the prosecutor's decision to charge, sentencing is another stage at which racial disparity is readily apparent. For example, Blacks are more likely to be charged under repeat offender laws—e.g., two- and three-strike laws. The racial impact of mandatory minimums is even more striking. More than 90 percent of those serving time for violating the federal crack law are Black or Hispanic. In 2000, 84.2 percent of the people sentenced were Black, 9 percent were Hispanic, and 6 percent were White.[33]

There have been numerous empirical studies on the effect of race on the outcome in death penalty cases. Most of the attention has been focused on the race of the defendant and the victim and on the interaction between these two factors.[34] However, very little attention has been given to the race of those on death row who are actually executed. Instead, the majority of studies focus on who receives a death sentence. Given that execution represents the ultimate case outcome, this postsentencing stage is a worthwhile area of inquiry. One study found that, while Blacks and Hispanics are most likely to be incarcerated for homicide offenses, Whites are more likely to be removed from death row and more likely to be executed.[35]

Felony disenfranchisement laws are a second example of how a law can have racially disparate outcomes. A 1997 report by the Sentencing Project found that the loss of voting rights as a result of a felony conviction has had a disparate impact upon Blacks and Hispanics. Overall, 4.2 million Americans are currently barred from voting while serving a felony sentence or have been permanently barred as a result of a felony conviction. Forty-seven states bar felons from voting while they are serving time. Twenty-nine states bar voting while on probation; thirty-two states bar parolees from voting; and fourteen states impose a lifetime bar on felons. The group hardest hit is Black men, who make up one-third of all felony disenfranchisement cases (1.4 million). Further, 13 percent of Black men of voting age are currently or permanently barred from voting.[36] In both Alabama and Florida, which bar current and former felons from voting, 30 percent of those barred are Black men.

As table 1-1 indicates, enactment of laws is one way that racial bias and discrimination proliferate. Justice system policies and practices are another mechanism. In some cases, they are unspoken directives. Whether measured or unmeasured, some justice system policies operate to allow law enforcement officials to disproportionately target minorities. The racial profiling of minority motorists is perhaps the best-known example of this problem. Studies done in New Jersey and in Maryland indicate that officers singled out Black motorists for traffic stops at rates far in excess of their rate of drug-related offending and rates of travel. As well, a Justice Department study of U.S. Customs found that Customs officers were nine times more likely to stop, frisk, and X-ray Black women travelers than White women travelers. Notably, White women were twice as likely as Black women to be found with contraband.[37] (For a detailed discussion of profiling, see chapter 6.)

In table 1-1, fetal endangerment refers to policies designed to identify and punish drug-addicted pregnant women. South Carolina's application of these laws offers a textbook example of how racially neutral laws can be applied in a racially discriminatory manner. In 1989, the Medical University of South Carolina implemented a policy that allowed staff members to secretly test pregnant women for substance abuse. The nonconsensual drug testing policy was designed to target pregnant women suspected of crack cocaine addiction.

The names of women who tested positive were given to the prosecutor's office. During the first year of the policy, with one exception, all of the women who were arrested and prosecuted by the solicitor's office were Black women. Interestingly, the case file of the lone White woman charged under the policy included a notation that she had a Black boyfriend. Also, the drug testing policy applied only to the Medical University, the only public hospital in Charleston and the one hospital with a predominantly African American patient population. Ten of the women charged under the policy filed a lawsuit arguing that the practice was unconstitutional. The U.S. Supreme Court agreed with them that the Charleston policy amounted to an unreasonable search and seizure in violation of the Fourth Amendment.[38]

There are a host of other decision-making practices and procedures within the justice system that are influenced by racial considerations. Table 1-1 lists some of these, including closed court proceedings, bench conferences, and the system's true black box—jury deliberations. As discussed, the language used throughout the process also presents a legitimate area of inquiry. Sheri Johnson's research indicates that an analysis of how race affects the court system mandates a consideration of courtroom language. This raises the issue of whether and to which degree this language influences judicial outcomes. Studies that examine the effect of race on judicial behavior also are cataloged here.[39]

All told, an evaluation of how criminal justice decisions are affected by race necessitates an evaluation of more than isolated stages of the process.

Laws, policies, and practices prior to arrest and after sentencing should be included in this analysis. Notably, the pre-arrest stage requires greater research attention since any extralegal race effect that occurs during this phase will directly impact who enters the justice system. In fact, the degree of racially biased decision making may be a significant factor in the number of minorities who enter and pass through the criminal justice process.

The above discussion outlines a preliminary typology for analyzing petit apartheid. It is offered as an important beginning step toward developing a complete schema for locations within the justice system wherein race-based decision making occurs. A fully realized typology would include all stages of the justice system, measured and unmeasured, prior to and following arrest and, for instance, a range of police policies and practices that might be influenced by racial considerations (e.g., use of excessive force).

V. Conclusion

This chapter makes two arguments. First, it suggests that mainstream assessments of how justice system decision making is affected by race are limited because they focus on only measured stages. To address these concerns, research on other stages, such as pre-arrest and postsentencing, should be included in assessments of how race affects justice system processing. Second, even within the measured stages, more research attention should be focused on how these studies can be expanded to consider decision-making processes and how they are influenced by race.

Georges-Abeyie's petit apartheid thesis serves as the foundation for these arguments. What makes his contribution novel is his contention that there are back regions within the criminal justice system where race consistently predicts outcomes. His articulation of petit apartheid offers an alternative analysis for measuring race effects. Specifically, Georges-Abeyie identifies several locations along the justice system continuum where racialized practices are business as usual. To many, these practices are invisible because they are not subject to official recordkeeping and do not involve overt racial discrimination.

One question raised by the petit apartheid analysis is whether it mandates measurement of all stages before any conclusions can be drawn about whether the entire system is influenced by race. In other words, must we engage in a microanalysis of *each* stage of the justice system, measured and nonmeasured, in order to draw any conclusions about the overall process? Or, can we allow some stages to serve as proxies for other stages? Researchers have attempted to draw conclusions about the process based on a few highly visible stages of the process. It is clear from the discussion that in order to avoid this problem, many more stages and processes need to be measured. Once this is done, it can be determined whether some stages may be representative of other stages.

A cursory sketch of some processes that lead to petit apartheid indicates that there are many locations and forms of race-based decision making. Future research should continue to explicate the typology—to include more forms of petit apartheid and to investigate how these forms course through the criminal justice system. Further, future work will need to consider the overall societal impact of race-based practices within the justice system, as well as their impact on specialized populations (e.g., young Black men). All told, what is needed is an analysis of the cumulative effects of petit apartheid practices on particular groups. To do anything less is to treat the criminal justice system's vise-grip hold on African Americans as an acceptable reality, rather than a social problem in need of redress.

2

American Indians and Crime
Invisible Minorities and the Weight of Justice

I. Introduction

The treatment that American Indians have received from the U.S. criminal justice system serves as a classic example of the harms and slights, intended and unintended, experienced by racial minorities within the criminal justice system. There are a host of injuries that go unnoticed and, therefore, unaddressed by the justice system. In fact, the experiences of American Indians, in society and in the justice system, represent a classic underground code.[1] Because the group's experiences operate mostly below the public radar, they are largely perceived and responded to in stereotypical terms. Many American Indians are processed and handled by a system that operates behind a legal curtain, which few social scientists have dared to pull back.

Each spring, thousands of undergraduate criminal justice majors graduate from U.S. colleges and universities. It is a good bet that few have been exposed to research, data, or discussion about American Indians and the criminal justice system. For those interested in learning more about American Indians and crime, there is little to draw from. Why is this?

First, when it comes to explicit examinations of race, the overwhelming focus of sociologists and criminologists has been on African Americans—who until recently were the largest racial group of color in the United States.

Second, American Indians make up a very small percentage of the U.S. population, less than 1 percent. According to the 2000 Census, approximately 2.5 million people identified themselves as American Indian. The number increases to 4.5 million if we add to it the number of people who said they were American Indian in combination with another race.[2] By either count, American Indians, who once numbered more than ten million, are the smallest racial group in America. Not surprisingly, there are very few American Indian academics, and only a handful with criminology doctorates. For example, between 1995 and 2000, fewer than five Native Americans received doctorates in criminology.[3] This is noteworthy because research indicates that minority criminologists are likely to study their own racial or ethnic group.

Third, for a variety of reasons, it is difficult to assess how Native Americans are processed through the criminal justice system. Native Americans are the one group whose criminal cases may be adjudicated in any one of three entirely separate legal systems—tribal, state, and federal. Even the most basic attempt to make sense of these schemes requires a broad knowledge base, one that includes history, law, criminology, sociology, and political science.

Individually and collectively, these factors help to explain the dearth of theories and analyses of Native American victimization and criminality in the United States. This chapter takes a small step toward bridging this gap and incorporates a range of information on American Indians and the justice system. The discussion centers on four themes. First, there is a consideration of foundational issues, such as how "American Indian" is defined. Second, there is an examination of some contemporary representations of American Indians. Third, and related to the former, there is a discussion of the use of American Indian names, mascots, gestures, and symbols within the mainstream. Fourth, there is an overview of the existing literature on crime and American Indians, legal and empirical. In conclusion, the silence on American Indian justice issues operates as an underground code—sending a subtle yet clear message that issues involving Indians and crime do not deserve widespread attention.

II. Choosing, Defining, and Locating

Before undertaking an analysis of the involvement of American Indians in the criminal justice system and how they have fared, it is necessary to address two preliminary issues. First, what is the appropriate racial label for the group commonly referred to as American Indians? Is it Native Americans? Aboriginals? Native peoples? Indians? Natives? Indigenous peoples? Is tribal affiliation appropriate? Are these terms interchangeable?

Are any of them *in*appropriate? Are there other terms that should be considered? These are important questions, because how a group is labeled may determine whether the group being studied will view the research as legitimate. Ideally, researchers would use the same name or names that the group being studied uses to describe itself. A 1995 study conducted by the U.S. Bureau of Labor Statistics found that "American Indian" was selected as the preferred term by half of those who identified themselves as either American Indian or Native American.[4] Thirty-seven percent of the respondents selected "Native American" as the preferred label, while 3 percent selected "Alaskan Native."[5] The absence of consensus on the choice of name has led some researchers to conclude that the group or person in question should be asked which racial label is preferred.[6] Given the results of the Labor Statistics poll, hereinafter either "American Indian" (sometimes abbreviated "Indian") or "Native American" will be used. For consistency, the racial labels used by researchers will be used when referencing their work.

Second, *who* belongs to the group labeled "American Indians"? Who is properly classified as an American Indian? There are several factors that complicate this question, including the fact that American Indians are a diverse group. The official government definition for an "American Indian" or "Alaskan Native" is "A person having origins in any of the original peoples of North and South America (including Central America), and who maintains tribal affiliation or community attachment."[7] As commentators have noted, this definition raises as many questions as it resolves. Further, there is no clear consensus across federal agencies and tribes. Eligibility for Bureau of Indian Affairs (BIA) services requires membership in a federally recognized tribe. Standards for tribal membership do not always comport with federal standards. For example, members of the Catawba tribe, a nonfederally recognized tribe, are eligible for some federal services and not others.[8]

Third, an important facet of this discussion requires a consideration of the unique cultural and spatial locations of American Indians. Most American Indians, almost 75 percent, do not live on tribal lands. Most live in rural, urban, or suburban areas. Approximately one-third of the American Indian population lives in Oklahoma, California, or Arizona. There are more than 515 BIA-recognized tribes.[9] Table 2-1 presents a picture of a group that is at once a part of the American mainstream and isolated from it.

III. *Face Forward: Cultural Portraits*

"noble" "earthy" "alcoholic" "spiritual"

An informal survey of undergraduates enrolled in a course on race, crime, and criminal justice at the University of Maryland indicates that many have stereotypical images of American Indians. The majority of the students enrolled in the course were White or African American. When asked to provide one-word summaries of contemporary representations of Native Americans, the following terms were typical: "noble," "earthy," "spiritual," and "alcoholic."[10] Over the five-year period (1998–2003) in which the course survey was taken, students' responses were consistent.

Students readily acknowledged having these stereotypes but indicated that they had little personal experience to refute these images. Their static impressions of American Indians are underscored by two points. First, there are sparse portrayals of Native Americans in popular culture. When asked, students were hard pressed to name either contemporary actors or fictional characters who are American Indian. The short list included Steven Seagal and Lou Diamond Phillips. Students also had difficulty naming television shows or movies with prominent American Indian

TABLE 2-1

American Indians: Some Statistics

- 2.5 million people selected "American Indian or Alaskan Native" as their race on the 2000 U.S. Census form.

- 4.1 million people selected either "American Indian or Alaskan Native" alone or with another race on the 2000 U.S. Census form.

- 43 percent of American Indians live in the West, 31 percent the South.

- California, Oklahoma, Arizona, Texas, and New Mexico are the states with the largest American Indian populations.

- 22 percent of American Indians live on reservations.

- The median age for American Indians is 28.7 years.

- 24.5 percent of American Indians live at or below the poverty line (800,000 people).

- The median annual household income for American Indians is $32,116.

Source: U.S. Census Bureau (2002), "The American Indian and Alaska Native Population: 2000" (February 2002).

characters. "Northern Exposure," "Dr. Quinn, Medicine Woman" (both canceled), and "King of the Hill" were referenced most frequently as television series with identifiably American Indian characters. In television's six decades, and over its thousands of programs, there have been few that feature an American Indian in a lead role. "Dances with Wolves" was commonly cited as a movie with leading American Indian characters. Students were also asked to name American Indians (besides actors) who are public figures, such as television personalities and politicians. This question drew blank responses. All told, students were not able to name five well-known American Indians who are actors, journalists, athletes, musicians, or politicians.

Second, public representations of American Indians are put forward primarily by people outside that racial group. That is, the mainstream portrayals of American Indians do not appear to be informed by interactions with or insights from Native Americans themselves. In the heyday of the cowboy/western movie, scores of stock stereotypical American Indian characters, shown primarily as the noble savage, were depicted on the silver screen. Into the mid-1960s, it was a common practice to have White actors portray American Indians.[11] Thus, in addition to being rarely seen, when American Indians were visible, it was typically via a White face, that is, through White representations of American Indian life and culture—a kind of racial ventriloquism.

Sherman Alexie's 1998 movie "Smoke Signals" stands as an exception to the mainstream portrayals of American Indian life. Alexie, a Spokane/Coeur d'Alene Indian, critiques Hollywood's staid images of American Indians. The small, independent film, however, could not be expected to compete with images and representations in Hollywood blockbusters, such as "Dances with Wolves."

Cultural Retreads: A Case in Point

The image of Native Americans as peaceful earth-worshipers is common. The *New York Times Magazine,* for example, frequently runs advertisements for the American Indian College Fund (AICF), which raises money for thirty-one tribal colleges.[12] The starkest of these shows a grainy lithograph-style portrait of a bare-chested American Indian man wearing tribal beads and a headband. Beneath his picture is his name, college, major (semiconductor manufacturing), and grade-point average (3.47).[13]

Another of these ads features an American Indian man standing in shallow ocean water, gesturing to a horse. In a third AICF print ad, an American Indian woman is shown performing a dance. The woman, who is dressed in traditional native regalia, appears to be in the desert. Each AICF ad features an early 1900s-style, black-and-white photograph.

It is not clear what to make of these advertisements. One interpretation is that they are a wink and nod: "We know how you envision us. So, we'll show you an image of us, albeit stereotypical, that you feel comfortable with. Send money now." Another is that the ads are to be taken seriously. They show American Indian college students in need of money to further their education. A third possibility is that the ads are both traditional and subversive. They offer a stereotypical, arguably nonthreatening, view of American Indians, using the standard representation of American Indian life to draw mainstream readers to the ad. Once there, readers are presented with a counterstereotypical view of an American Indian—one who is pursuing a college education.

Perhaps none of these three interpretations is accurate. Perhaps more than one is accurate. Given that there are so few visible portraits of American Indians, it is reasonable to critique the few that appear, especially those that appear in publications with a large number of subscribers. Had these ads appeared in a low-circulation publication, their impact would be questionable. The *New York Times Magazine,* however, has a readership of rainmakers—an elite group of American movers and shakers who determine which racial images will be thrust into public view. Further, the same ads have appeared in other upscale publications, including *The New Yorker* magazine.[14]

Interestingly, the AICF uses a radically different ad in *Honey,* a hip-hop fashion magazine that targets young, urban, Black females. Here, the AICF ad, in color, features a young American Indian woman, casually dressed in a white shirt and black jeans. She appears to be in an elementary school classroom. Behind her is a large shelf, where microscopes are stored. A small child's hand can be seen pulling at the young woman. The text reads, "Have you ever seen a real Indian?" The placement of such diverse ads raises the questions of why and what it means that a traditional and stereotypical portrait of American Indian life is presented to the elite, white readership of the *New York Times* magazine, while an entirely modernized depiction is presented to *Honey* readers, who are primarily young, African American women.[15]

Sticks and Stones

Attempts by Native Americans to shape their own public image continue to be downplayed by other racial groups. Specifically, other groups appear to place little value on how Indians label themselves. The best-known contemporary example of this phenomenon is the use of American Indian names for athletic team names and mascots.

Scores of professional, collegiate, high school, and middle school athletic teams have American Indian names.[16] At the professional sports level, for example, there are the Atlanta Braves, Chicago Blackhawks, Cleveland Indians, Kansas City Chiefs, and Washington Redskins. The use of American Indian names for athletic team names is not limited to any particular sport or region of the country. Additionally, a number of teams use American Indian mascots and songs.

For years, American Indian groups and individuals have argued that these names are offensive caricatures of their culture, race, and ethnicity. Indian groups have employed various measures to challenge the use of these names and images. There have been lawsuits, protests, hearings, and boycotts. In 1999, a group of American Indians filed a lawsuit against the Washington Redskins. They argued that the team's name is offensive and should be changed. The federal action was brought under the Lanham Act, which prohibits the use of any trademark that disparages people, institutions, beliefs, or national symbols or "brings them into contempt or disrepute."[17] For some Indians, the term "redskin," which references the genocide of American Indians, is particularly offensive. It is their "N" word. It describes the practice, engaged in by Whites during the American frontier era, of hunting down and killing "red skins" (Indians) and offering their scalps as evidence of death for the bounty payment.

In a novel argument, one legal researcher states that the use of Indian names or words as part of athletic team names violates Title II of the 1964 Civil Rights Act. This provision guarantees everyone, regardless of race, color, religion, or national origin, the "full and equal enjoyment" of public places, which includes sports arenas and stadiums. It is argued that American Indians are deterred from attending sporting events when one (or more) of the teams has a racially offensive name. If this is true, Native Americans are not free to enjoy public sports arenas in the same way that members of other racial groups are able to enjoy them. The researcher concludes that sports stadiums are closely connected with their teams and their team names and that therefore racially derogatory team names violate the Civil Rights Act.[18]

The public response to these objections generally ranges from disinterest to denial that the names cause any type of affront. Some have even suggested that the decision to use Indian names is a sign of respect. For example, Daniel Snyder, owner of the Washington Redskins, has said that the team name "honors" Native Americans.[19] Arguably, the credibility of this statement and others is challenged when we consider what the public outcry would be if teams were to use names that were racially offensive to Blacks or Jews. In his discussion of this issue, Randall Robinson offers some stinging examples: "Washington Blackskins," "New York Jews," and "Atlanta Mafia." He concludes: "When the victims are small in number, peripheral and voiceless . . . even when the hurt is completely gratuitous, [it] contributes to costly social disintegration, and lengthens the distance between us as Americans."[20]

This last point is underscored by the 1999 incident involving John Rocker, a former pitcher for the Atlanta Braves. Rocker made several racially charged remarks in an interview published in *Sports Illustrated*. He launched a verbal attack against numerous individuals and groups, opined that Asian women cannot drive, and referred to one of his Black teammates as a "fat monkey." Rocker's broadest racial scorn, however, was reserved for foreigners:

> I am not a very big fan of foreigners. You can walk an entire block in Times Square [New York] and not hear anybody speaking English. Asians and Koreans and Vietnamese and Indians and Russians and Spanish people. . . . How the hell did they get into this country?[21]

In response to Rocker's tirade, Major League Baseball (MLB) insisted that he get a psychological examination. The Rocker episode received widespread press attention. At one end of the continuum, the response was, "We may not like Rocker's speech, but he has a First Amendment right to exercise it," at the other end, "He's a racist."

Regardless of the position one takes on how the Rocker incident was handled, the irony of the MLB sanction is hard to miss. At the same time that Rocker was sanctioned for his harsh racist remarks against racial minorities, the Atlanta Braves permitted—in fact, encouraged—the display of gestures, logos, and name calling that some American Indians find offensive. In 1987, the Atlanta Braves reintroduced the tomahawk hatchet as part of their logo. In addition to the large tomahawk logo, Braves fans have an Indian call—a chant that can be heard at Turner Field throughout home games. Adding insult to injury there is the "tomahawk chop," which appears to be a cross between a ceremonial offering and a cheerleading maneuver. Together, the logo, chant, and the Indian call demonstrate how American Indians are viewed and celebrated. An editorial cartoon aptly satirizes the contradiction; in the cartoon, a Braves fan, a man, is wearing a T-shirt that says, "Do the Tomahawk Chop!!" and a button that says, "Go Braves. Scalp 'em." The Braves fan, who is explaining the Rocker incident to a young child, is saying, "Son, John Rocker was what we call 'racially insensitive.'"[22]

There is an additional, subtler irony in the handling of the Rocker affair. It appears that a racial slur used by an individual against a group may be rebuked and sanctioned. However, slurs or epithets that have been incorporated into the social fabric are apparently permissible. It is odd that it is socially unacceptable to utter racial slurs against some minority groups but not others. This brings to mind the concluding scene of George Orwell's *Animal Farm*. In the final battle over rights, the powers-that-be conclude: "All animals are equal. But some are more equal than others."[23] The absurdity of the some-are-more-equal-than-others argument may simply be a numbers game. One journalist, Eugene Robinson, rhetorically asks, "What is it except numbers [of American Indians in the United States] that makes [some] names unacceptable, but Indian-derived names just fine?"[24]

In response to concerns raised by Native Americans, several college teams have changed their names. For example, in 2001, Southwestern College retired its thirty-seven-year-old nickname, "Apache."[25] As well, some states, including Maine, Montana, and Colorado, have enacted laws to change racially derogatory geographical names. In 1995, Minnesota became the first state to pass a law that requires renaming any body of water with the word "squaw," which is a crude reference to female genitalia, roughly equivalent to "cunt."

A natural point of comparison is the public's response to slurs considered racially offensive to American Indians and the response to those considered slurs (e.g., the "N" word) to African Americans. It is widely accepted that the "N" word is racially charged and should not be used, at least publicly. Non-Blacks, particularly Whites, face public censure for use of the word, regardless of context or intended meaning.[26] For many Native Americans, "squaw" and other caricatures used to depict Indian life amount to racial slurs that are comparable to the "N" word for African Americans. However, American Indian slurs—which, notably, Indians do not use as terms of endearment—are not accorded the same public sensitivity. The reasons for the different responses are varied. First, as noted, there are relatively few American Indians; thus, the voices of protest are muted. Their small population makes it easy to dismiss the use of these names as harmless fun. Second, in general, there is a widespread ignorance about Native American history, cultures, and mores. In sum, the debate over Indian terms raises a twist on the classic conundrum: If a tree falls in the forest when no one is there to hear it, has it made a sound? Applied to American Indians, if they speak, yell, and holler that they do not wish to be called certain names or reduced to particular labels—ones they consider racial slurs—yet few listen, have they spoken?

IV. Legal and Empirical Overview

At least one commentator has referred to the justice system that applies to American Indians as a "jurisdictional maze."[27] The following discussion underscores this characterization. The legal process for Native Americans is largely controlled by six federal statutes.[28]

- *General Crimes Act* (1854). This legislation removed from federal jurisdiction crimes committed by Indians against non-Indians in Indian country. Specifically, it applies to those who are subject to punishment by local (tribal) law.
- *Major Crimes Act* (1885). This Act gave U.S. federal courts the power to adjudicate select crimes—those occurring in Indian country. The statute applies where the offender is an American Indian (the victim may be of any race). The enumerated crimes include murder, manslaughter, kidnapping, rape, incest, assault with intent to kill, assault with a dangerous weapon, arson, burglary, and larceny.
- *Assimilative Crimes Act* (1898). This Act provides that state law governs on federal property (e.g., Indian reservations) where state law cannot be enforced. It applies only to interracial crimes involving an Indian and a non-Indian. It is designed to enhance uniformity by avoiding the creation of a double standard of criminality for state residents and federal personnel.

- *Public Law 280* (1953). This statute terminates federal oversight of tribal lands. The law transfers civil and criminal jurisdiction to the state where the reservation exists. The law applies to California, Minnesota, Wisconsin, Nebraska, Oregon, and Alaska.
- *Indian Civil Rights Act* (1968). The Act provides for the adoption of U.S. constitutional guarantees by tribal courts (those that hear criminal cases). Procedural guarantees include the right to counsel and the privilege against self-incrimination.
- *Indian Self-Determination and Educational Assistance* (1975). This federal law allows tribes to decide whether to use the BIA police or to create their own tribally controlled police force.

As this list indicates, there are three basic factors to consider when determining which court has jurisdiction over a case involving an American Indian: the location of the crime; the race of the victim and the offender; and the applicable law. An initial consideration is whether the offense took place inside or outside Indian country. Generally speaking, crimes that occur within Indian country are heard by tribal courts. Next, it must be determined whether state law applies. If the offense took place in Indian country, the applicable law is ascertained by considering the race of the victim and the offender.

Grasping even a cursory understanding of these separate systems and their points of overlap is complicated. The multilevel jurisdictional scheme presents a daunting task for the criminal justice researcher whose goal is to understand how American Indians are processed and treated by justice systems within the United States. In addition to the complexity of the federal statutes, tribal court sovereignty has slowly eroded. These laws, combined with others, have chipped away at Indian self-determination, specifically, the ability of Indians to determine what constitutes a crime and what constitutes appropriate sanctions. The hodgepodge of federal laws limit tribal court jurisdiction.

Department of Justice Report on American Indians and Crime

The combination of the three-tiered system of justice for Indians (tribal, state, and federal) and the fact that most of the crime research on race labels American Indians as "Other" make it impossible to offer definitive statements about American Indians and crime. Not surprisingly, much of the existing research focuses on particular subgroups within the American Indian community (e.g., a particular tribe or state). However, a 1999 report by the Justice Department comes close to providing a comprehensive and contemporary portrait of the American Indian experience within the U.S. criminal justice system, both as offenders and as victims. The forty-one-page study is based upon data collected between 1992 and 1996.[29] It includes data collected by the U.S. Census, the FBI, and the Bureau of Justice Statistics. There are several notable findings:

- American Indians have the highest rates of violent victimization. Between 1992 and 1996, their rate was 124 per 1,000 people in the population. This is more than twice the rates for Blacks (61) and for Whites (49). It is four times higher than the rate for Asian Americans (29). A look at the figures by race and gender indicates that the rate of violent victimization for American Indian women (98) is higher than the rate for Black men (56).
- American Indians have the highest rate of interracial victimization. Indians are most likely to be victimized by someone who is not Indian. As a rule, most crimes involve an offender and a victim of the same race. Seventy percent of the offenses committed against American Indians, however, involve a non-Indian offender. Sixty percent are estimated to be White offenders, and 10 percent are Black.[30]
- American Indian offenders are more likely to have been under the influence of drugs or alcohol at the time the crime was committed, than are offenders from other racial groups. Fifty-five percent of American Indian victims said the offender was under the influence of drugs or alcohol, compared with 44 percent of White victims, 35 percent of Black victims, and 25 percent of Asian American victims.[31]
- Four percent of American Indian adults are under the control of the criminal justice system. This rate is twice as high as the control rate for Whites (2 percent) and approximately nine times higher than the rate for Asian Americans (less than one-half of 1 percent). Blacks have the highest control rate (10 percent).

These findings are alarming. First, the victimization rate for American Indians, a racial group that constitutes less than 1 percent of the U.S. population, is very high. Second, the control rate for American Indians, 4 percent, is very high. In actual numbers, there are approximately sixty-three thousand American Indians within the control of the criminal justice system. More American Indians are under the control of the justice system than are Asian Americans. This is remarkable given that the total population of Asian Americans is approximately four times that of American Indians.

Third, researchers have looked beyond conviction rates to consider sentence length. This is an important issue for American Indians, who are more likely to be subject to federal jurisdiction than are members of other racial groups. As a rule, federal sentences, which are governed by the federal sentencing guidelines, are longer and stricter than either state or tribal court sentences. Under the updated Indian Civil Rights Act, tribal court sentences cannot exceed one year in jail or impose more than five thousand dollars in fines. On average, federal sentences are typically two to four years longer than state sentences for the same offense. Further, at the federal level, "good time" reductions have been limited, and parole has been abolished. American Indians are disproportionately more likely to live on federal land; thus, those who are arrested are disproportionately likely to be charged with violating a federal law. And, those who are convicted are more likely to receive longer sentences. All told, American Indians are more likely to receive longer sentences than are members of other racial groups. In 1997, American Indians made up almost 2 percent (1,817 prisoners) of the federally incarcerated population. Thus, they were overrepresented in federal prison, where they were held at a rate equal to twice their proportion of the general population.[32]

This reality also works a harsh injustice on American Indian youth. One legal researcher, Amy Standefer, argues that the application of the Federal Juvenile Protection Act unfairly penalizes Native American juveniles.[33] Standefer observes that the Act's automatic transfer provisions allow it to be used in ways that thwart its designed goal of removing juveniles from criminal prosecution. For instance, in 1997, 137 Native American juveniles entered federal prison. This compares with thirty-four White juveniles, thirteen African Americans, and five Asian Americans who entered federal prison the same year. Standefer reports that in some years Native American youths have made up 61 percent of the juvenile population in the federal system.

In addition to jurisdictional mandates that place American Indians at a relative disadvantage, researchers have pointed to other possible explanations for these racial disparities. These include microlevel (e.g., learning, social control) and macrolevel (e.g., conflict) theories. Unfortunately, very little empirical research on these theories has been completed, and most of what exists is state-, county-, or tribe-specific and, thus, the findings cannot be generalized to American Indians as a group. Overall, however, researchers have concluded that American Indians are subject to discrimination and unfavorable treatment within the U.S. justice system.[34]

V. Conclusion: For the Future

A relatively small number of researchers focus on Indian criminal justice issues. This group includes American Indian activists, historians, criminologists, sociologists, and legal researchers. Notably, the Justice Department has launched several initiatives designed to study American Indians and justice-related issues.[35]

As this chapter's cursory discussion makes clear, several problems plague the study of American Indians and the criminal justice system. First, American Indians are subject to varied and complex jurisdictional rules and statutes. Second, their population is geographically diverse. A sizable percentage of American Indians live on reservation lands, a large number live in rural areas, and others reside in urban centers. Depending on their state and area of residence (combined with other factors, including race of the victim and the offender), some Indians are subject to federal laws, others to state laws, and still others to tribal laws and customs. Third, American Indians are a racially heterogeneous group. Data from the 2000 Census indicate that 22 percent of the more than six million respondents who selected more than one racial category were American Indian and White. Fourth, with a population of less than three million, American Indians make up less than 1 percent of the U.S. population. Their small numbers may partly explain the widespread ignorance concerning their experiences within the criminal justice system. All told, these factors make it difficult yet imperative to present a comprehensive portrait of American Indians' interaction with the criminal justice system.

The complicated and illogical patchwork of legal designations and pronouncements applicable to American Indians makes it nearly impossible for the casual observer to comprehend their contemporary plight. The above discussion unequivocally supports the need to focus more research attention on American Indians and the criminal justice system. This should include more detailed, focused research on American Indians at the tribal, state, and federal levels. The ultimate goal should be to provide a fuller portrait of American Indians and the justice system. This will enhance the probability that responsive and workable policies will be implemented. Hopefully, the existing code of silence around American Indians—the least populous racial group and a group with one of the highest rates of victimization in the United States—will end.

3

Gangsta Rap and Crime
Any Relationship?

I know it when I see it.
                    —Justice Potter Stewart (1964), U.S. Supreme Court[1]

I. Introduction

In the early and mid-1990s, rap music faced its most prolonged and acute attack to date. By then, rap music, almost twenty years old, had become a popular music choice for American youth and a multimillion-dollar industry—an urban Rumpelstiltskin tale, life's harsh reality spun into gold. It had become a popular music choice for American youth of all races. This time, however, the attack could not simply be dismissed as the angry voices of those who did not understand the lyrics or those who had been against it since its inception. These critics focused their energy not on rap music per se but rather on one of its increasingly marketable forms—"gangsta rap."

The challenge to gangsta rap began as part of an attack on heavy metal music, initiated by the Parents' Music Resource Center (PMRC). Tipper Gore led a successful charge to have parental advisory warning labels placed on sexually explicit and violent recordings. The PMRC, made up primarily of congressional wives, sought to examine and report on the lyrics of heavy metal and rap music.[2] The group's efforts, though successful in raising public awareness and winning the use of mandatory record labeling, faced numerous challenges. Some dismissed the PMRC as a group of out-of-touch, self-righteous zealots promoting censorship. This characterization of the PMRC may have been a result of a generational divide between its supporters and its opponents, a reaction to the perception that PMRC used strong-arm tactics to achieve its goals, or a response to the group's direct and familial access to members of Congress.

A consideration of what constitutes gangsta rap offers some understanding as to why it has ignited such controversy. A review of articles and books makes clear that there is no uniform definition.[3] Like obscenity, it is in the eye of the beholder. Justice Potter Stewart's pronouncement on obscenity, applied to gangsta rap, would likely be, "I know it when I hear it." Though there is no standard description of gangsta rap, there are a series of interrelated themes that are present in the music and that consistently emerge in discussions of this art form. Gangsta rap includes music that:

- Uses crude terminology to refer to women or female anatomy
- Glorifies gang activity
- Expresses hatred, dislike, or frustration with law enforcement
- Brags about the use of firearms
- Celebrates the use of marijuana or other drugs
- Professes sexual prowess and domination
- Encourages criminal activity
- Portrays a prison sentence as an expected, routine fact of life.

Other issues as well are explored in gangsta rap. It presents, for example, the harsh realities of urban life, such as crime, neglect, and despair. The above list, however, highlights those topics that set gangsta rap apart from other forms of rap music.[4]

The intense scrutiny of gangsta rap offers a unique opportunity for evaluating the intersections of race, class, and crime—the tacit, coded message of a presumptive link between gangsta rap and crime. This chapter explores these purported connections. It examines the confluence of events that moved gangsta rap to the front burner of social issues. Next, there is a discussion of the ways in which rap music has been integrated into mainstream American culture. The third section looks at the steps taken, legal and congressional, to control the expanse of the music. The fourth part evaluates the empirical research on the relationship between gangsta rap and deviance. This is followed by an analysis of how this music has been represented within the mainstream press and popular culture.

The intrinsic value of gangsta rap and its sociopolitical consequences are important topics for discussion and critique. There are legitimate criticisms that some of this music is misogynistic, sexist, and vacuous. As well, questions have been raised as to whether it perpetuates stereotypes of African American youth as highly sexualized and criminal. These issues are important and in some instances overlap with the focus of this chapter—whether there is a relationship between gangsta rap and crime.

II. Mobilizing Events

In the 1990s, the release of four records mobilized the opponents of gangsta rap: N.W.A.'s "Fuck tha Police" (1988); 2 Live Crew's "As Nasty as They Wanna Be" (1989); Ice-T's "Cop Killer" (1992); and Tupac Shakur's "2Pacalypse Now" (1991). Though there had been earlier criticisms of rap music, the response to gangsta rap signaled a concentrated and sustained effort, one that could not be ignored. While buffered by the early work of the PMRC, the anti–gangsta rap movement was initiated primarily by law enforcement officials, who feared the music would lead to physical assaults against its rank and file.[5]

The 1989 release of 2 Live Crew's album, "As Nasty as They Wanna Be," caused a firestorm of controversy. The furor over the recording brought into sharp focus what had become the core issues surrounding whether gangsta rappers have a right to make music, have it played, and have it heard. This case was propelled into the national spotlight after a Broward County, Florida, sheriff obtained a court order stating that the album was obscene. Store owners and managers were threatened with arrest if they continued to sell the rap group's album. What followed was a high-profile criminal case in which competing cultural experts, including Henry Louis Gates, weighed in on the artistic merits of the music. Gates argued that the lyrics reflected longstanding Black cultural traditions and had artistic value.[6] The court, however, found that the recording, replete with sexually explicit lyrics, was obscene.[7]

"Fuck tha Police" triggered an FBI investigation. One FBI official wrote a letter to N.W.A.'s label, denouncing the album and stating that it "encourages violence against and disrespect for . . . law enforcement."[8] The letter went on to detail the number of police officers who had been killed in the line of duty. As well, officers around the country began a fax campaign designed to track the whereabouts of N.W.A. members.

Opponents of Ice-T's "Cop Killer" brought to bear the experience of earlier anti–gangsta rap efforts. The song, which appeared on the album

"Body Count," describes one man's plan to kill police officers. Once it began to receive air play, the lyrics were condemned by political forces, ranging from the Reverend Jesse Jackson to former vice president Dan Quayle. Sixty members of Congress signed a letter to Warner Brothers stating that the song was despicable and vile. California's attorney general sent a letter to music store chains, requesting that they discontinue sales of the disk. Under mounting pressure (following canceled concerts and corporate threats to sell Warner Brothers' stock), Ice-T had the song removed from his album.[9]

Tupac Shakur's "2Pacalypse Now" offers the other bookend for early gangsta rap records that proved controversial. Shakur's record also received attention when it was offered as part of a criminal defense in a murder case. In 1992, Ronald Ray Howard, a nineteen-year-old Black man, was arrested and charged with killing Bill Davidson, a Texas state trooper. Howard had been pulled over for driving with a missing tail light. During the stop, Howard "snapped" and killed Davidson with a nine-millimeter pistol. At the time, Shakur's cassette was playing in Howard's tape deck. Howard's attorney argued that Shakur's antipolice lyrics had inspired Davidson's murder. One of the songs, 'Soulja's Story," includes the following lyrics:

> Cops on my tail, so I bait till I dodge them
> They finally pull me over and I laugh,
> Remember Rodney King
> And I blast his punk ass
> Now I got a murder case . . .
> . . . What the fuck would you do?
> Drop them or let them drop you?
> I choose droppin' the cop![10]

The jury was not persuaded by the argument that Shakur's gangsta rap music compelled Howard to commit murder. He was found guilty of capital murder and sentenced to death.[11]

Links continue to be made between gangsta rap music and crime. One example of this is found in the 2002 Washington, D.C., area sniper killings. There was early speculation that the defendants, John Muhammad and juvenile Lee Boyd Malvo, had used gangsta rap lyrics to chart their murderous course. Specifically, it was thought that the two had been urged on by the lyrics of the gangsta rap group Killarmy.[12] While it remains unclear whether gangsta rap music played any role in the sniper shootings, it is noteworthy that the genre was readily linked to the crimes.

During the same period that these four controversial recordings were released, there was rising public concern with juvenile crime rates. In particular, a growing number of states and municipalities expressed alarm at the perceived increase in gang-related activity. Some linked this to the rise in school shootings and to the influence of gangsta rap.[13] In response, some jurisdictions enacted antigang legislation.

These cases illustrate the widespread concern that gangsta rap has generated and continues to generate. The notoriety of these cases is largely responsible for the widespread condemnation of gangsta rap music. The next section considers the ways in which rap music has become more mainstream and at the same time has been closely associated with deviance. Rap lyrics, combined with the prominence of controversies involving gangsta rappers, have led some to presume the existence of a link between listening to gangsta rap music and involvement in criminal activity.[14]

III. Rap Life

It is no surprise that the public sees a continuous thread joining rap music, rappers, gangsta rappers, and crime. An April 1999 Gallup Poll found that six out of ten teenagers said that listening to gangsta rap music causes violence.[15] The prevalence of rap music, its portrayal, its integration into American culture, and the actions of some rappers explains the interest in, scrutiny of, and alarm about gangsta rap. The discussion below considers some factors that explain the widely held perception that gangsta rap is both prevalent and criminogenic.

Prevalence. Two factors contribute to the perceived omnipresence of gangsta rap. First, for the uninitiated, rap and gangsta rap are lyrically indistinguishable. For some people, hearing music that sounds like a series of loud, angry, run-on sentences may be enough to justify a "gangsta rap" label. The words are often spoken in rapid-fire, high-decibel, difficult-to-decipher prose. Thus, for some people, rap music *is* gangsta rap music. From this view, gangsta rap may appear to be more prevalent than it actually is.

Second, rap and hip-hop culture have increasingly become part of mainstream American youth culture. One indication of this is the proliferation and commercialization of rap-related accessories and cultural products. This includes fashion designers who have dedicated themselves to outfitting the hip-hop generation. For example, there are clothing labels (e.g., Phat Farm, Sean Jean, FUBU, Roca-wear, Iceberg, Encye, and Esco) and clothing lines (e.g., Tommy Hilfiger, DKNY, and J-Lo) that promote the hip-hop style. Additionally, there are rap and hip-hop magazines (e.g., *Vibe, Source,* and *XXL*). Further, rap-style lyrics are regularly heard on TV and radio commercials, from the Super Bowl to Nick-at-Nite. Notably *Billboard Magazine*'s weekly list of the top ten songs regularly features rap music selections. In another line-blurring twist, the Princeton philosopher Cornel West recorded a rap record.[16] As well, today's youths view tattoos as a type of cultural expression. Interestingly, tattoos, the body art de rigueur for rappers, have historically been associated with marginal cultures (e.g., ex-convicts and Hells Angels).

Further, the culture of hip-hop, which includes rap music, has created an interesting alliance among celebrity, professional sports, and rap music. Notably, some high-profile young Black male athletes have sought rap careers (e.g., Shaquille O'Neal, Kobe Bryant, and Allen Iverson).[17] In another twist, one gangsta rapper, Master P, actively pursued a professional basketball career. Also, there have been several high-profile athlete-rapper connections, such as the professional relationship between Heismann-trophy winner Ricky Williams and his manager Master P, and the friendship between the former NFL cornerback Deion Sanders and the rapper M.C. Hammer. All told, the lines that separate rap, gangsta rap, culture, and celebrity have been blurred. This may make it hard for some people to distinguish between rap and gangsta rap; they, therefore, treat them as one and the same.

Crime Inducing. One reason for the presumed link between gangsta rap and crime is how the music is visually portrayed. Gangsta rap is one of the few music forms to emerge since the advent of music videos. As a result, rap fans may be hard pressed to differentiate between the lyrics of gangsta rap and the visual images of gangsta rap. The issue of prevalence and the perceived criminality of gangsta rap also overlap. Gangsta rap may appear to be more widespread given that other forms of music (such as pop and hip-hop) utilize some of the same images—the baggy pants, the affected macho swagger, the gangster pose, the simulated strip-club dancing by scantily clad, voluptuous women, and the jarring photographic techniques.

In addition, because more than a few rappers have had well-publicized run-ins with the law, there are legitimate reasons to ask whether there is a connection between gangsta rap and crime. Many have been arrested for, charged with, and in some instances convicted of criminal activity. The list includes some of the biggest names in rap music: Sean "P Diddy" Combs, Da Brat, DMX, Dr. Dre, Jermaine Dupri, Flava Flav, Jay-Z, Juvenile, Mystikal, Ol' Dirty Bastard (Osirus), Raekwon, Redman, Tupac Shakur, Shyne, Slick Rick, Biggie Smalls, Snoop Doggy Dog, and Suge Knight. The association between rappers and criminal behavior may be made even where there is no evidence of a link. This occurred in the wake of the October 2002 shooting death of Jam Master Jay (Jason Mizell), a member of the pioneering rap group Run-DMC. Some attempted to link his murder to the violence in gangsta rap lyrics. Mizell, however, was a family man and community activist, not a gangsta rapper.[18]

The self-portrait presented by some gangsta rappers may cause some people to link the music with crime. For instance, some gangsta rappers proudly espouse a criminal culture and make no apologies for the subjects they rap about or the lyrical content of their songs. They stress that they are "keepin' it real"—portraying hard-knock urban life in verbal, living color. As well, some gangsta rappers served time before beginning their rap careers, and some have made records detailing their criminal past. It is this latter group that appears to represent the general public's image of all gangsta rappers.

This section has assessed the connections that link rap music, gangsta rap and mainstream culture. The music has not only created controversy; it has also motivated political responses. The next section reviews the congressional and legislative reactions to gangsta rap.

IV. Calling on Congress

The bound, interlocking images of crime and gangsta rap music have been seared into the public consciousness. Amazingly, the perceived threat of gangsta rap—based on no hard facts—has been so widespread that it has evoked a complex and vast array of official responses. Artists and promoters of gangsta rap have been threatened with a daunting combination of legal, political, economic, and criminal sanctions. This includes corporate divestiture, corporate boycotts, FBI investigations, and congressional hearings.

The breadth of the response is demonstrated by the strange political bedfellows who joined forces to abolish gangsta rap. Perhaps the oddest alliance was that between C. Delores Tucker, head of the National Political Congress of Black Women, and William Bennett, a conservative activist. In the late 1990s, the duo launched a campaign to have corporate boards held accountable for financing the production of gangsta rap music. Tucker summarized this strategy as follows:

> We are talking about establishing guidelines for more responsive and responsible corporate citizenship. A corporation must be granted authority by a governmental body in order to exist. No corporation should be allowed to exist if it engaged in activities that contaminate and infect the minds of children. We protect whales, we protect owls, we protect rivers. There are already laws in existence that protect children from child pornography and exploitation, but not from purchasing this music.[19]

In 2003, it was revealed that Bennett was a decade-long, high-stakes gambler. Ironically, Bennett, whose estimated losses top $8 million, was affiliated with an industry associated with moral decline and known for its links to organized crime.

Additionally, the Reverend Calvin Butts, of the Abyssinian Baptist Church, in New York, has been an outspoken critic of gangsta rap music. In 1993, Butts launched a crusade against gangsta rap. He led boycotts against stores that sold the music. At one demonstration, he used a steam roller to crush hundreds of offending compact disks. The political and social prominence of the proponents and opponents of gangsta rap forced the issue into the political spotlight. At the height of the controversy, the topic was fodder for the Sunday morning television talk shows.

In response to the loud objections to the music, Congress organized two separate hearings. In 1994, the subcommittee on juvenile justice held hearings on the impact of music on children. The panel, "Shaping Our Responses to Violent and Demeaning Imagery in Popular Music," was organized by then-senator Carol Moseley-Braun.[20] Various witnesses testified, including C. Delores Tucker; Michael Eric Dyson, a professor; Ron Stallworth, a Utah police sergeant; Laura Murphy Lee, of the ACLU; Robert Phillips, of the American Psychiatric Association;

Dionne Warwick, a singer; Maxine Waters, a member of the House of Representatives, from California; and then-senator William Cohen, of Maine.[21] No definitive conclusions were reached at this hearing. For the most part, witnesses offered their perspectives on gangsta rap music, focusing on how the lyrics affect young people. Several, including Waters, made the point that the music reflects the all-too-real experiences of youths in the nation's urban ghettoes: "It is not the words being used. It is the reality they are rapping about."[22] Some panelists, including Tucker, offered anecdotal links to violence. Most steered clear of asserting a direct tie between gangsta rap and crime. However, speaking to the press after the hearings, Moseley-Braun stated that some gangsta rap has a "causal relationship" to street crime and violence.[23] In view of the panel's title and its promise to address violence in popular music, it is unclear why the hearing focused almost exclusively on gangsta rap music.

In 1997, Congress held another hearing, "Music Violence: How Does It Affect Our Children?"[24] This panel's goal was to list steps that record labels could take to prevent objectionable music from getting into the hands of young people. Six witnesses testified: C. Delores Tucker; Frank Palumbo, of the American Academy of Pediatrics; Hilary Rosen, then-president of the Recording Industry Association of America; Donald Roberts, a professor; Raymond Kuntz, a parent; and Kent Conrad, a U.S. senator from North Dakota. In contrast to the 1994 hearing, the focus extended beyond gangsta rap. Panelists referred to musicians from other genres, including Guns N' Roses and Marilyn Manson. Witnesses expressed concern about increasingly vulgar and explicit music lyrics.

Along with the congressional scrutiny of gangsta rap, some corporations were reconsidering their role in promoting vile lyrics.[25] In September 1995, following mounting public criticism of the lyrical content of gangsta rap, particularly the music of Snoop Doggy Dog and Tupac Shakur, Time Warner sold 50 percent of its stake in Interscope Records. There were also challenges to entities that held stock in companies that produced rap music. At least two states have considered such legislation. For instance, in Texas, legislation was introduced to prevent government pension funds from investing in companies that promote offensive music. In 1998, then–Texas governor George W. Bush signed the bill into law. The following year, however, a court overturned legislation that prohibited state-funded investments in companies that manufacture or distribute music that degrades women or promotes violence.

The next section evaluates the empirical research on the relationship between rap music and crime. This provides a broader context for analyzing the actions of Congress, specifically, whether the congressional concern about the deleterious effects of gangsta rap music are in accord with the empirical data.

V. *Empirical Research*

Very little of the professed angst about gangsta rap has translated into research that examines whether there is a link, direct or otherwise, between listening to gangsta rap music and becoming involved in crime. While there have been hundreds of newspaper and magazine articles and TV news stories warning of the deleterious effects of rap music, fewer than twenty research articles devoted to the topic were published between 1990 and 1999. Only a subgroup of these studies specifically address gangsta rap. An even smaller group actually tests the hypothesis that gangsta rap *causes* crime. All told, there are few research studies on this controversial issue. This absence is particularly striking given that, within mainstream discourse, the tacit assumption appears to be that there is some relationship between gangsta rap music and deviance. What follows is an overview and assessment of the existing research. This research and the discussion that follows are divided into four broad categories: the impact of gangsta rap on criminal behavior; its affect on antisocial (not necessarily criminal) behavior; its influence on overall attitudes and perceptions; and its link to other social problems.

Impact on Criminal Behavior. In a 1999 study, Susan Gardstrom examined the connection between exposure to rap music and criminal offending from the viewpoint of male felony offenders.[26] Gardstrom's research is based upon a survey of ninety-seven males who were housed at a residential facility for convicted youth offenders. The participants, who ranged in age from twelve to seventeen years old, were asked twenty-six questions about the impact of their music preferences on their attitudes and behaviors. More than three-quarters (77 percent) of the youths said that rap was their favorite type of music. On average, the participants said they listened to three hours of music each day. Fewer than 17 percent of the youths said the music had any effect on their overall mood. Six percent stated that listening to rap music led to involvement in criminal activity. These findings offer little support for a link between rap music and crime.

In another 1999 study, Stuart Fischoff assessed the link between rap music and crime.[27] The trial of a Black man charged with murdering his girlfriend was used as the backdrop for this research. The defendant had been found guilty of first-degree murder. Violent gangsta rap lyrics written by the defendant were used as character evidence by the prosecution. Fischoff created a study to determine how potential jury members would view someone who not only listened to gangsta rap music but wrote his own lyrics. In particular, he sought to examine whether potential jurors believe that someone who listens to gangsta rap music is more likely to engage in criminal offending than someone who does not listen to the music.

A total of 134 White, Asian American, Hispanic, and Black college students participated in the study. After the students were randomly assigned to one of four conditions, each one was given a hypothetical case and asked to assess the personality traits of the main character. Each scenario involved a Black male high school senior who was also a state track champion. In one variation, the young man wrote gangsta rap lyrics and was charged with murder. In another, he wrote gangsta rap lyrics but was not charged with murder. In a third version, he did not write gangsta rap lyrics and was charged with murder. In the final variation, the young man neither wrote gangsta rap lyrics nor was charged with murder. For the first and second variations, participants were provided with written lyrics.

Fischoff found that the study participants were much more likely to attribute negative characteristics to someone who writes gangsta rap lyrics. Specifically, they were more likely to view such a person as selfish, sexually aggressive, unlikable, and involved in gang-related activity. Further, the findings indicate that participants had more negative reactions to the lyrics than to the murder charge. Fischoff's findings do not establish a relationship between gangsta rap and crime. His research, however, supports the view that gangsta rappers themselves (and those who write their lyrics) are perceived in negative terms.

Attitudes toward Crimes against Women. In a 1995 study, the researchers Christy Barongan and Gordon Nagayama Hall evaluated whether misogynous rap music impacts sexual aggression against women.[28] They randomly assigned fifty-four college students (all male, mostly White) to one of two groups. The first group listened to misogynistic rap music, the other to neutral rap music. After listening to approximately fifteen minutes of music, the participants were then asked to rate the songs they had heard. Following this, they watched three short videos. One film showed a conversation between a man and woman. The second involved sexual violence (e.g., a woman's shirt was ripped off by the man), and the third clip showed a man being physically aggressive toward a woman. After viewing these vignettes, the participants were asked to select one of the films to watch with an unknown woman.[29] Those participants who had listened to misogynous rap music were much more likely to select the clip involving sexual violence than those who had listened to neutral rap music. These findings suggest there is a relationship between listening to misogynistic gangsta rap and receptivity to viewing sexual violence. Again, however, this does not establish a causal connection between listening to gangsta rap and committing crime.

A 1995 study by James Johnson, Lee Jackson, and Leslie Gatto examines the link between exposure to rap music and attitudes.[30] The researchers surveyed forty-six members of an inner-city Boys' Club. The Black youths, ages 11 to 16, were randomly assigned to one of three groups. Groups one and two were told that they would participate in two separate experiments. The first part involved watching music videos (approximately twenty-four minutes total) followed by an assessment of how the participants stored information. Group one was shown eight violent videos; group two was shown eight nonviolent videos.[31] The second part involved reading two passages, followed by an assessment of the participant's decision-making abilities. The third group, the control, did not watch any videos. Its members were told that their decision-making skills would be evaluated on the basis of their reading of several passages and answering related questions. Scenarios were read by participants in all three groups. The first involved a violent act by a man against a woman, and the second involved a conversation between a young man in college and his friend. The male friend is unemployed, yet owns expensive material possessions.

Johnson and his colleagues found that youths who were exposed to violent rap music reported a greater acceptance of violence than those who either saw nonviolent videos or were in the control group. In addition, youths who were exposed to violent rap music videos were more likely to state that they would engage in similar actions. Finally, compared with participants in the control group, those who were shown the videos (violent and nonviolent) were more impressed with the "materialistic" young man than with his financially strapped college friend. On the basis of this research, Johnson and his colleagues conclude that "rap music may play a role in violent behavior among African American males."[32] These findings indicate that youths who listen to violent rap music are more receptive to violence. Though these findings offer some support, they do not establish that listening to violent rap music results in violence.

In 1993, Bruce Wade and Cynthia Thomas-Gunner conducted a study on the influence of gangsta rap on attitudes toward rape and sexual assault.[33] They examined whether college students who prefer gangsta rap over other forms of music are more likely to be tolerant of sexual assault and whether those who prefer explicit music lyrics are more likely than others to minimize its impact. Fifty-nine students, mostly Black, participated in the survey. The researchers found that students who preferred gangsta rap had attitudes that were significantly more supportive of rape and sexual assault. Also, women were more likely to indicate that explicit lyrics are misogynistic and can lead to aggression against women. Overall, 80 percent of the students stated that gangsta rap leads to aggression against women.[34] These findings provide support for the view that youths who prefer gangsta rap are more accepting of antifemale aggression. They do not establish causality—whether those who listen to the music already had antifemale attitudes or whether they developed those attitudes after listening to gangsta rap music.

Impact upon Mood. Mary Ballard and Steven Coates conducted a study to examine whether listening to rap and heavy metal music affects one's mood. Their findings are based upon data gathered from 175 college students (94 percent White). Students were divided into two groups, heavy metal and rap. Within these groups, students were assigned to listen to nonviolent, homicidal, or suicidal music lyrics. Each group heard approximately thirty seconds' worth of music. Afterward, students were queried about the lyrical content and about their mood. The researchers found that lyrical content did affect the immediate mood of the participants. However, there was no indication of any long-term effects. Specifically, students who listened to rap music were more likely to have an angry mood than those who listened to heavy metal music. Ballard and Coates note that most participants stated a preference for rock music, and some may have been bothered by having to listen to rap music. This study provides qualified support for the view that listening to rap music may negatively affect one's short-term mood.

Other Social Problems. In a 1994 study, the researchers Kevin Took and David Weiss examined the relationship between "adolescent turmoil"[35] and listening to heavy metal and rap music. Their findings are based upon questionnaires completed by eighty-seven adolescents, ages 12 to 18. Sixty-two percent of the participants were White males. The participants were outpatients who had been assigned to a military medical center, psychiatric center, counseling service (for substance abuse), or private psychiatric hospital. Took and Weiss hypothesized that if listening to aberrant music causes psychosocial problems, this would be reflected in their subject population.

The researchers collected data on music preferences and participant demographics (e.g., grades, drug use, and sexual activity). On the basis of the adolescents' music preferences, Took and Weiss divided them into three groups—heavy metal, rap, and "others." They found that youths who preferred heavy metal or rap music experienced greater social problems, such as behavior problems and low grades. They also found gender effects: The majority of the participants who stated a preference for rap or heavy metal were male. As the authors note, the behaviors they found to be associated with those who listen to heavy metal and rap may simply reflect the behaviors associated with adolescent males, who were the majority of the study's participants.

In 1990, Jonathon Epstein, David Pratto, and James Skipper analyzed the relationship between musical preference and behavioral problems. The sample consisted of eighty children (ages 11 to 16) who attended an alternative middle school. Sixty-six percent of the participants were Black, and most were young men. Epstein and his colleagues tested three hypotheses: whether music preferences were tied to racial group membership, whether music preferences predict behavioral problems, and whether the amount of time spent listening to music is positively related to behavioral problems. For the first hypothesis, they found strong support. Ninety-nine percent of Blacks indicated a preference for rap, and 96 percent of Whites indicated a preference for heavy metal. The preference for pop music was equally divided by race. Though one-third of the sample had experienced behavioral problems, there was no support for the second hypothesis. There was also no support for a link between the number of hours a participant listened to music and the probability that he would have behavioral problems.

Analysis of the Research. Based on the above research, there is no evidence of a causal link between gangsta rap music and crime. Overall, the literature is too sparse to allow us to draw any broad conclusions. Further, the research designs leave the most important question— whether listening to gangsta rap causes criminal activity—unanswered. What follows is an overview of eight concerns raised by the existing studies.

- *Comparative Analyses.* There is a need for more research that compares the effects of various forms of music on attitudes and behaviors. Absent comparative data, it cannot be determined whether there is a specific relationship between listening to gangsta rap and involvement in deviant behavior or a more generalized relationship between listening to particular forms of music (e.g., heavy metal, gangsta rap, or country) and involvement in deviant behavior. Given that rap music is a global commodity, an international look at the affect of gangsta rap on behaviors and attitudes of non-American youth would allow for comparisons with American youth.
- *Race of Rappers.* It is important to empirically assess whether and how rappers' race is relevant to the perceived threat and mainstream reaction to gangsta rap. Specifically, are White gangsta rappers, such as Eminem, subject to the same kind of criticue as Black and Latino gangsta rappers?[36] A related issue is whether the scrutiny of gangsta rap is comparable to the scrutiny given to other music genres, such as the music of predominantly White musicians who use crude lyrics (e.g., heavy metal).
- *Impact of Music Videos.* An assessment of the impact of gangsta rap necessitates a look at the influence of music videos. This would allow for a distinction to be made between the effects of viewing music videos and listening to the music and the effect of just listening to the music. An analysis of the role of visual mediums in shaping attitudes and influencing behavior is particularly important because they may be the primary source of exposure for some populations (e.g., adolescents).

- *Cross-Racial Samples.* Studies should include more racially diverse groups. For example, research should include Asian Americans, Hispanics, and Native Americans, who make up approximately 20 percent of all American youth.
- *Selection Bias.* To avoid selection bias, studies should not be limited to select populations (e.g., youths at medical facilities or group homes). Samples drawn from larger, more representative populations enhance the generalizability of research findings.
- *Expanded Hypotheses.* The existing studies on gangsta rap are designed to assess the music's negative effects. Research hypotheses, however, could be expanded to address other, more positive, outcomes, such as whether the music acts as a catharsis or serves as a form of political expression.[37]
- *Longitudinal Studies.* Assessments of the effect of gangsta rap on crime should include research that examines individuals over a period of time (e.g., as adolescents, teenagers, and adults). Longitudinal studies would provide insight into those people who listen to the music and do not engage in crime and those people who listen to the music and do engage in crime.
- *Criminals versus Noncriminals.* Studies on people who have been involved in criminal activity and listen to gangsta rap music can help us assess the impact of listening to gangsta rap on offending. This can be compared with the impact of gangsta rap on those who listen to it but who have not been involved in crime.

These eight points draw a road map for future research on the effect of gangsta rap music on criminal offending. The unavoidable conclusion to be drawn from the existing research is that it does not establish that gangsta rap causes crime.

VI. Racializing Culture

Cultural critic bell hooks contends that the attack on gangsta rap has followed a predictable pattern: "A central motivation for highlighting gangsta rap continues to be the sensationalist drama of demonizing black youth culture in general and the contributions of young black men in particular."[38] She forcefully argues that an analysis of gangsta rap cannot be carried out in the absence of an understanding of the culture in which it is produced. Hooks finds a direct link between the sexism and misogyny in gangsta rap and the sexism and misogyny in society at large. Thus, she concludes, gangsta rap is neither subversive nor a departure from the mainstream; it is an "embodiment of the norm."[39]

Other commentators support this assessment. Referring to the assault on gangsta rap, Tricia Rose states:

> The more public opinion, political leaders, and policymakers criminalize hip hop as the cultural example of a criminal way of thinking, the more imaginary black monsters will surface. In this fearful fantasy, hip hop style . . . becomes a code for criminal behavior, and censuring the music begins to look more like fighting crime.[40]

As well, Kimberlé Crenshaw observes that gangsta rap is threatening to many Whites because it appears to celebrate the "Black male as outlaw."[41] These analyses lend support to the argument that a tacit, unspoken link is being made between gangsta rap and crime, specifically, that, by using coded language, the reaction to this music has been similar to the reaction to other expressions of Black culture—a fear of criminality and deviance.

Compared with other forms of contemporary controversial music, gangsta rap has received the lion's share of scrutiny and condemnation. In a detailed assessment of the media prisms through which race is viewed, Amy Binder analyzes how rap music has been portrayed by the print media. In a 1993 article, she compares coverage of gangsta rap in mainstream media accounts (e.g., the *New York Times, Newsweek,* and *Reader's Digest*) and in Black media outlets *(e.g., Ebony* and *Jet* magazines). Binder identifies several "frames" that are used by the press to discuss and report on heavy metal and rap music. These include "protection," "corruption," "danger to society," "generation gap," "freedom of speech," and "threat to authorities."

Binder reports that both heavy metal and rap were most frequently framed as "danger[s] to society."[42] Mainstream articles, however, were significantly more likely to describe rap music fans as dangerous—e.g., "the legions of misogynistic listeners who pose a danger to women."[43] Further, mainstream articles were more likely to note the negative effect of rap music upon society at large. When discussing heavy metal, mainstream media reports focused on the harm to its listeners; by contrast, their coverage of rap music focused on the harms to society at large.

Binder found that the two Black media outlets included in the study were more likely to conclude that rap is "not harmful."

A 1996 study by Carrie Fried supports Binder's work and provides an intriguing test of the impact of media coverage on perceptions of rap music. Fried's research explores whether it is rap music lyrics that cause a negative reaction or whether it is the artists' race that explains people's negative perceptions of the music. Fried observes that rap music, "viewed as a predominantly Black form of music, may be judged through the tainted lens of a Black stereotype, which includes such traits as violence, hostility, and aggression."[44] The study, divided into two parts, looks at whether songs identified as rap are more likely to receive a hostile response than other types of songs (e.g., country and folk).

The first set of findings is based upon the responses of 118 randomly selected Whites. They were asked to read the first verse of "Bad Man's Blunder," a folk song originally recorded by the Kingston Trio in 1960. The song tells the story of a young man who searches for and kills a police officer:

> Well early one evening
> I was rolling around
> I was feeling kinda mean
> I shot a deputy down
> I rolled along home
> and I went to bed
> I laid my pistol
> up under my head
>
> Chorus:
> Well, I rolled along home, I took my time
> And I went to bed, I thought I'd sleep some
> I laid my pistol, a big .22
> Up under my head, I like to keep it handy.[45]

Participants were not informed that "Bad Man's Blunder" was performed as a folk song. Depending upon which survey form they received, participants were told that the song lyrics were rap, country, or folk. Next, they were asked to evaluate the lyrics, including their degree of offensiveness, their likelihood of causing a riot, their dangerousness to society, and whether such lyrics should be regulated. The results revealed a consistent pattern. Those who were told that the lyrics were for a rap song were significantly more likely to report a negative response on all measures than were those who were told that the lyrics were for a country or folk music song.

The second part of the study used similar methods. The only change was that participants, in addition to being asked to read the song lyrics, were shown a picture of the artist. Those selected for one group were shown a picture of a young Black man, while those in the second group were shown a picture of a young White man. In both pictures, the artist had short hair and was wearing a sports coat over a T-shirt. Eighty Whites participated in the second part of the study. On all measures, the findings were similar to those of the first study. Fried concludes:

> [T]he race of the singer play[s] a significant role in reactions to musical lyrics. The same lyrical passage, which is acceptable as a country song or when associated with a White artist, becomes a dangerous, offensive song in need of government regulation when it is a rap song or associated with a Black artist.[46]

The Binder and Fried studies underscore the readily made link between rap music, race, and deviance. Notably, their research findings reflect the widespread perception that rap music creates or attracts a loathsome group of listeners. Further, it indicates that some people object to the *sound* of the music. In some ways, the response to rap music is reminiscent of how some earlier forms of Black music were dismissed as not legitimate (e.g., be-bop and blues). Many believed these genres attracted unsavory musicians and fans.

VII. *Conclusion*

As a genre, rap music and its 1980s and 1990s incarnation, gangsta rap, has become popular culture's black sheep. It has been treated to an enduring, broadside attack by the public, politicians, musicians, and clergy. As detailed in this chapter, gangsta rap's opponents posed a formidable challenge. Despite rap's popularity, or perhaps because of it, however, the protests have obscured some important questions.

There appears, however, to be more to the concern about gangsta rap music than meets the ear. The intense focus on gangsta rap says as much about the protestors as it does about the music itself. The heavyhanded condemnations have largely missed the opportunity to consider why gangsta rap developed as an art form and why it continues to have resonance for so many youths, particularly African Americans. As well, the attacks on the music have lacked a historical context. Leola Johnson comments:

> The campaign to silence gangsta rap . . . faced a conceptual problem. While every group professed to be interested in limiting lyrics that could incite antisocial acts, each group's view of which acts should be targeted was skewed by race and class considerations. The police, for example, ignored the misogyny in gangsta rap lyrics and fought solely against songs that portrayed aggressions against police. [T]he National Political Coalition of Black Women . . . worked solely against misogyny in rap, ignoring the rampant misogyny in other black institutions such as the church.[47]

The rush to judge the music's long-term affects in the absence of empirical support suggests that something more was afoot. Related to this, many have argued that gangsta rap has been subjected to greater scrutiny than other forms of controversial music.[48] The name itself, "gangsta" rap, implies criminality. Notably, there is no music genre with a comparable label, such as "gangster rock."

A legitimate question about the ethical value of gangsta rap music appears to have been fused—and confused—with a causal relationship to criminal activity. A hypothesis about the music has been offered in the form of statement. There is a wide gulf between the dismissal of gangsta rap as a deviance-inducing art form and empirical data. The research simply does not support a direct link between listening to gangsta rap music and involvement in crime. One does not have to be a fan of the music to agree with Public Enemy's rallying cry, "Don't believe the hype."[49]

4

Policing Communities, Policing Race

Lamont: Did you know that diabetes and heart disease are the
leading killers of blacks?
Fred: I thought it was the police.
—*Sanford & Son*, TV Show (c.1973)

I. Introduction

Many people can remember the first police brutality case that made them
sit up and take notice. For some, it was a national case, such as the one
involving Amadou Diallo, Abner Louima, or Rodney King. For others, it
was a local case. Like clockwork, every few years, our first brush with police brutality is linked with a contemporary case of police abuse. These
cases, new and old, force us to ask ourselves, individually and collectively,
a range of questions: Did the police go too far? Were they provoked?
What constitutes excessive force? And, what are the appropriate sanctions for police violence?

With each incident, national and local, the public expresses shock
and dismay. When prosecuted, cases wind their way through the legal
system—ultimately arriving at their final resting place, dusty legal annals. These incidents reveal the layers and the complexity of police brutality. Given this, it is not surprising that many of the core issues associated with the topic—intricate and historically laden—have eluded sustained social discussion and comment. There is a haze, thick and
oppressive, that surrounds police brutality and appropriate, workable
policy responses. The first goal of this chapter is to cut through this fog
by charting a road map through the current discourse on police brutality. The second goal is to identify and challenge concepts that have been

passed off as established facts about police abuse, to illuminate the undercode codes of police violence.

This chapter, which examines the covert link between police abuse and race, is divided into six sections. The first part examines how police abuse has come to be defined as a "Black" social problem. This section also addresses how the problem of police brutality is framed so that minorities, Blacks in particular, are blamed for the problem. The second part evaluates the statistics and the empirical data on police brutality and citizen assaults against police. The third section examines the historical relationship between the police and African Americans. The fourth part describes the police brutality "dance"—the social, political, and legal maneuvers applied in most well-known incidents of police abuse. The fifth part assesses the societal impact of continuing to apply a business-as-usual strategy to the problem of police brutality, and the sixth section is the conclusion.

II. *"It's a Black Thing"*

In the 1980s, there was a controversial, popular slogan among college-age Black youth: "It's a Black thing, you wouldn't understand." This in-your-face declaration was emblazoned on t-shirts, baseball caps, and buttons worn by African Americans. The slogan concisely summarizes the public representation of police brutality. Specifically, it has been treated as a problem that uniquely faces members of the Black community—a problem for which Blacks are held responsible. Further, it has been framed as a problem that does not concern Whites as a community. This racial distancing is not unique to the issue of police brutality. Once a Black face is placed on a social issue, there are a series of predictable, yet ineffective public responses; depending upon its "racial baggage," a social issue may invoke sympathy or scorn.

For example, most people readily associate affirmative action with African Americans. Likewise, discussions of race and crime almost never center on Whites and crime; they typically refer to Blacks or Latinos and crime. This racial reductionism is nowhere more apparent than in media portrayals of welfare. The popular perception and representation is that millions of poor, lazy Black people are draining the nation's coffers through monthly welfare checks. Each of these topics—affirmative action, crime, and welfare—has acquired its own racial baggage. Once an issue becomes "a Black thing," something that is readily (and negatively) identified with Blacks and Blackness, it is treated as a social problem that threatens democracy. Such problems are frequently met with harsh legislation or ignored by social scientists and policymakers.[1]

The affirmative action debates of the 1990s offer the best example of this. Once affirmative action was characterized as a set-aside for Blacks, it was increasingly perceived as a threat to Whites. The fact that White women are and have been the primary beneficiaries of affirmative action programs carried no measurable weight in the public discussion. In addition to the debates about the need for "color-blind" legislation, myths and anecdotes that told of unqualified minorities who had taken jobs away from qualified Whites were circulated. Many Whites, we are to believe, have a friend or relative who has lost out on jobs or promotions (to which they were entitled) because their potential employers had to hire or promote undeserving Blacks. A little thought, however, unmasks this argument as a numerical impossibility. How, in fact, could Blacks, who make up approximately 12 percent of the U.S. population, be responsible for "taking" jobs away from White men, who constitute close to 35 percent of the U.S. population?

The process of recasting broad social issues as Black-only problems represents an empirical perversion. A similar phenomenon appears to be at work with police brutality. What was once a generic term used to describe police abuse against citizens has come to symbolize a confrontation between members of minority communities and the police.

Simply put, the public face of a police brutality victim is that of a young man who is Black or Latino. One cost of racializing police brutality as "a Black thing" is that the problem cannot be embraced as a broad social issue, one that everyone has a stake in resolving. The racialization of police brutality may lead some to conclude that there is something unique about Blackness that explains and justifies police abuse. This sends a subtle message that there is a causal link between Black skin and police assaults and an even subtler, coded, underground message that police abuse can be ignored.

In Search of the White Rodney King

There is no nationally known White victim of police brutality. This conundrum is highlighted by the query "Where is the White Rodney King?" Even in the absence of a White poster child for police brutality, where are the White victims on the local evening news? Is it possible that none exist?

This is implausible when we consider that each year Whites account for 67 percent of all arrests. There are few statistics available on the incidence and prevalence of police brutality by race. Existing figures indicate that White arrestees are more likely to be the victims of police force than Black arrestees; Blacks, however, are disproportionately victimized by police brutality.

The public is less likely to hear about brutality cases involving White victims. There are several possible explanations for this, including: (1) Police abuse directed against White victims is much less likely to raise issues of racism; (2) police assaults against Whites are less severe than those against Blacks; (3) Whites are less likely than Blacks to report incidents of police abuse; and (4) Whites are less likely than Blacks to label police assaults as "brutality"; therefore, these cases are less likely to attract widespread media attention.

The Gidone Busch case underscores this point. On August 30, 1999, the emotionally disturbed Busch was shot and killed by six police officers in New York City. The police had responded to neighbors' calls that Busch was praying loudly. The officers said that when they arrived, Busch attacked them with a hammer. In response, they fired at him eleven times, killing him. News reports about the case centered on Busch's mental illness. Though the media made explicit references to Busch's religious faith, Orthodox Judaism, little attention was focused on his "Whiteness." The case was neither labeled nor treated as an incident of police brutality. In a later case, a White man was beaten by White police officers in Georgia.[2] The incident, captured on videotape, shows a man who had been stopped for drunk driving. The case, which stirred little public comment, was not labeled "brutality."

The fact that there are so few White names linked to police brutality underscores and explains how racialized the issue has become. People sympathize with victims who look like them. Reginald Denny was a White victim of random violence in the aftermath of the acquittal of four White LAPD officers charged in the captured-on-videotape beating of Rodney King. Denny's case is illustrative of White allegiance to and sympathy for an innocent White victim of the violence that followed the verdict. At the time of the assault, Denny was driving a cement truck through the intersection of Florence and Normandie in South Central. Denny, who was attacked by a group of young Black men, viciously beaten, and left for dead, was widely, and justifiably, embraced as the innocent victim of a violent, random assault.

There are, however, stark differences between Denny's assault and the police assault of someone Black. The Rodney King and Reginald Denny cases are noteworthy because they highlight how differently Blacks and Whites perceive threats of random violence. Whites fear being victimized by random street violence at the hands of minority thugs. Blacks, on the other hand, fear being the random victims of police violence.[3]

These racial realities highlight the difficulty of making the problem of police brutality a cross-racial issue, a concern that everyone has a stake in resolving. What would it take to get Whites as a group to take on the issue of police brutality? It is easy to envision the public outcry and concern if there were five separate incidents involving shootings of innocent Whites by Black officers. In the same way that the Littleton, Colorado, high school massacre sparked national interest in and action to prevent school violence, a spate of White victims of police assault would likely be a catalyst for substantive policy responses to the problem of police abuse. Such a scenario, however, is unlikely.

Although Whites as a group do not view police brutality as an issue of major concern, some Whites do see it as a potential threat. The March 8, 1999, issue of *The New Yorker* magazine suggests a blurring of the lines between Whiteness and police brutality. The cover drawing shows a White New York City police officer at a shooting gallery. His gun, however, is not aimed at the usual suspects. It is pointed at three White citizens, a businessman talking on a cell phone, a small boy eating an ice cream cone, and an elderly woman hobbling along on a cane.

The New Yorker cover came on the heels of the Amadou Diallo shooting case. In February 1999, Diallo, a Guinean immigrant, was shot and killed by four members of the NYPD. Police wrongly suspected the twenty-two-year-old of rape. Undercover officers approached the unarmed Diallo as he stood in the vestibule of his Brooklyn apartment building. In response to their approach, Diallo raised his wallet. The police, who mistook the billfold for a gun, shot and killed him. In effect, *The New Yorker* cover suggests that, in view of the number of cases involving Black victims, Whites, too, should be fearful of the NYPD.

Blaming the Victim

Not only has police brutality been widely defined as a Black problem; it appears to be a problem for which Blacks are responsible. This sleight-of-hand reasoning mirrors arguments that have been offered to justify police practices that target minority citizens, such as "DWB" ("driving while Black"). Some suggest that the disproportionately high levels of police abuse against Blacks and Latinos can be explained by their high rates of offending. Put another way, police brutality against Blacks and Latinos is excusable as a by-product of their high rates of involvement in crime.[4] The reasoning is as follows:

1. Blacks are disproportionately involved in street crime.
2. Police reasonably suspect that Blacks are involved in street crime.
3. Therefore, it is reasonable that Blacks are disproportionately stopped by the police. Blacks, then, have a greater probability of being victims of police brutality.[5]

An unstated assumption of this deduction is that the high rate of Black offending gives the police a legitimate basis for fearing, stopping, and assaulting Black citizens. There are several problems with this line of reasoning. For starters, the argument is circular: Blacks have high rates of crime, therefore high rates of police abuse. The nexus between these two, however, has not been empirically demonstrated. For example, there is no evidence that the level of police assaults against Blacks increases and decreases on the basis of the rate of Black offending. Further, according to this reasoning, the majority of Blacks are required to pay the debt incurred by the small percentage of the group who are offenders. This perspective is not so much an argument as it is a way of shifting blame. This defensive chess move forms the core of arguments that place the blame for police brutality upon its victims, who happen to be disproportionately Black. Further, this approach sends a message to Blacks that unless they reduce their rate of offending, they can expect to be victims of police brutality.[6] As applied to police brutality, this reasoning would require that Blacks alone shoulder the burden of solving the problem of police abuse (see section III for a discussion of the amount of contact between citizens and the police). It also encourages police strategies that use race as an indicator of criminality.

The Good Victim. An interesting phenomenon operates along with the racial finger pointing that permeates discussions of police brutality—The "good" victim requirement. As some well-known cases demonstrate, not all victims of police assault are viewed in a sympathetic light. There are several characteristics that define a "good" victim of police assault. A "good" victim is employed; has graduated from high school; has no prior criminal record; has neighbors or colleagues who speak well of him; and appears nonthreatening. Victims with one or more of these attributes appear to have the best chance of being labeled "good" and thus deserving of public sympathy.

The Amadou Diallo case offers a textbook example of the good victim phenomenon. As noted earlier, Diallo was shot and killed by New York police, who mistook him for a rape suspect. Following Diallo's death, the public learned that he was a hard-working immigrant from a two-parent family. Despite Diallo's "good" victim status, however, the four officers charged in his death were acquitted of any wrongdoing.

At the other end, the case involving Patrick Dorismond illustrates what can happen when one is not designated a "good" victim. In March 2000, less than one month after the Diallo acquittal, undercover New York officers approached Dorismond, a security guard, outside a Manhattan night club. Police, who were engaged in an undercover drug operation, asked the twenty-six-year-old Dorismond where they could purchase drugs. A scuffle ensued, and Dorismond was killed by police.

In an attempt to show that Dorismond did not deserve the public's sympathy, then-mayor Rudolph Giuliani, after Dorismond's death, permitted the release of his sealed juvenile criminal record.[7] The message was clear: Dorismond was a "bad" victim, not worthy of public support. The posthumous leak of Dorismond's closed file appeared to be calculated to evoke sympathy for the officers involved in the shooting. This new information encouraged the public to believe the impossible—that, at the time of the shooting, the officers were aware of Dorismond's juvenile record (his prior criminality) and, therefore, justifiably threatened by him. The illogic of this message was never directly challenged. Instead, the image of Dorismond as a bad man—a bad victim—prevailed. The grand jury declined to issue indictments against the officers involved in Dorismond's death.

As these cases indicate, the good victim–bad victim dichotomy unfairly places a burden on the victim—or, in some instances, on his survivors—to prove the victim's worthiness. Such reasoning shifts attention away from the behaviors and practices of police officers.

The good victim phenomenon has some parallels to what happens in some rape cases. In some sexual assault cases, attempts are made to use the victim's sexual past to determine whether a "real" rape occurred. In some instances there are disclosures of the victim's sexual history (e.g., promiscuity). Rape shield laws, however, were enacted to bar this kind of evidence. Notably, these prohibitions do not work in the court of public opinion. Information about the victim of police brutality is initially heard in the same way that information about a victim of rape may be initially heard.

In the Diallo and the Dorismond cases, the police were operating undercover. The victims had no way of knowing whether they were being approached by police officers, robbers, or thugs. This is a little-discussed, though critical, aspect of both cases. From this perspective, the victims' reactions to the approaching men could be viewed as reasonable. This is particularly noteworthy given the rote responses many Black men have in encounters with the police. Commentators have observed that Black men, in an attempt to de-escalate potentially tense encounters with the police, have adopted a range of nonthreatening behaviors. This conduct includes keeping their hands in plain view, as well as using a deferential tone and manner when addressing police officers.[8] The behavior of Diallo and Dorismond is directly at odds with this response—thus indicating that they did not know they were being approached by the police.

III. Use of Force by and against the Police

A review of government data on the use of force by and against police officers adds an important perspective to the discussion of police assault and brutality. Two government surveys collect national data on the use of force by the police. First, the Police-Public Contact Survey (PPCS) provides a snapshot of police-citizen encounters.[9] It is based upon interviews with a nationally representative sample of U.S. residents age 16 and older.

Several interesting findings emerged from the 2001 PPCS report. First, approximately 21 percent of the respondents said they had had contact with a police officer in 1999. "Contact" includes being stopped for a traffic violation, reporting a crime, asking police for assistance, witnessing a traffic accident, or being questioned as a crime suspect. Of that 21 percent, 1 percent reported that their encounters with the police involved the threat or actual use of force. "Force" includes pushing, grabbing, kicking, hitting, spraying with chemicals, or shooting a gun. Fifty-nine percent of the encounters that involved force or threats of force were directed at White residents, and approximately 23 percent were directed at Black residents. Thus, Blacks are disproportionately more likely than

Whites to experience a police encounter that involves the use of force. Second, Whites have the highest police contact rate. Each year, approximately 22 percent of Whites have contact with the police. The figures are 19 percent for Blacks and 16 percent for Hispanics. Third, 20 percent of Whites surveyed said their encounter resulted in an injury, while 8.2 percent of Blacks reported an injury. Fourth, in approximately 25 percent of the police-citizen encounters, the respondent indicated that he had done something to provoke the police.

The second government survey, "Policing and Homicide, 1976–98" (P&H), details incidents of justifiable homicide by police and incidents involving police who were killed by felons.[10] The study reports annual averages for the twenty-two-year period. On average, police kill four hundred felons each year, and, on average, felons kill seventy-nine officers each year. Extrapolating from this 400:79 ratio, it appears that, between 1976 and 1998, officers killed felons at a rate five times higher than the rate at which felons killed police officers.

The survey reports several notable findings. First, Whites constitute the majority of felons who are killed by the police. As table 4-1 indicates, 56 percent of felons killed each year are White, and 42 percent are Black. In recent years, Blacks have made up a declining percentage of justifiable police homicides. For example, in 1998, Whites accounted for 62 percent of justifiable deaths, and Blacks constituted 35 percent.[11] Second, a look at the data by age shows that young Black men ages 13 to 24 are overrepresented as victims of police homicide. They make up 1 percent of the U.S. population and 14 percent of those killed by police. Their rate is almost six times higher than the rate for young White men. Young White men are represented as homicide victims at a rate (15 percent) proportionate to their rate in the overall population (14 percent).[12]

Third, the P&H survey found that most of the law enforcement officers who either were shot by a felon or killed a felon were White.

TABLE 4-1

Felons Killed by Police and Police Killed by Felons,
Percent by Race, 1976–1998 (Averages Reported)

	Percent of Felons Killed by Police	*Percent of Felons Who Killed Police*
Black	42%	43%
White	56%	54%

Source: Department of Justice (2001), "Policing and Homicide, 1976–98: Justifiable Homicide by Police, Police Officers Murdered by Felons," p. iii.

Specifically, 84 percent of the officers who killed felons were White, and 86 percent of the officers who were killed were White.[13] Most of the felons who killed police officers were White (54 percent), and 43 percent were Black.

Table 4-2 presents a racial breakdown of the findings for the P&H study. As indicated, most killings by police and most killings of police are intraracial; that is, most involve an officer and a felon of the same race. In 62 percent of the cases where an officer was killed, both the officer and the felon were White (52 percent) or both the officer and the felon were Black (10 percent); the majority involve a White officer and White felon. In 65 percent of the cases involving the killing of a felon, both the officer and the felon were White (53 percent) or both the felon and the officer were Black (12 percent). The figures for interracial killings indicate that cases involving a White police officer who was killed by a Black felon represent 28.5 percent of police killings; cases involving a Black felon killed by a White officer make up 29.6 percent.

While the data reported in the homicide and policing study are valuable, questions remain. First, the report does not indicate the number of citizens who are killed each year by law enforcement officials. The study was confined to police killings that involved felons.[14] Notably, the study uses a broad definition for "felon"—it refers to someone who is an actual

TABLE 4-2

Race of Police Officer Killed and Race of Felon Killed,
by Race of Killer, 1976–1998

	Race of Officer Killed	
	Black	White
Felon's Race		
Black	10%	28.5%
White	2.4%	52%
	Race of Felon Killed	
	Black	White
Officer's Race		
Black	12%	3%
White	29.6%	53%

Source: Department of Justice (2001), "Policing and Homicide, 1976–98: Justifiable Homicide by Police, Police Officers Murdered by Felons," pp. 12, 26.

or a "suspected" felon.[15] Thus, in this report, a "felon" would include a person with a clean record (e.g., Amadou Diallo) or someone who had been convicted of a misdemeanor. Second, the study is limited to deaths classified as "justifiable" by the police department. Whether a police killing is "justifiable" is determined by individual police agencies. Third, the report does not indicate whether the police officer was in uniform or operating undercover. This information is particularly relevant in cases where the police kill citizens. It raises the question whether the victim knew that he was being approached by law enforcement (e.g., the Diallo and Dorismond cases). Interestingly, the report provides statistics on the number of incidents in which a uniformed police officer was killed: 72 percent of the officers killed were wearing their uniforms. The reverse data, however, are not available. In an evaluation of police shootings of civilians and police shootings by civilians, it is relevant to consider whether the police officers were in uniform or in plainclothes.[16]

Fourth, national level data mute the high rate of police killings in some jurisdictions. For instance, a 1998 study by the *Washington Post* found that the District of Columbia leads the nation in police shootings.[17] Between 1994 and 1997, D.C. officers killed forty-three citizens. During this same time period, the findings indicate that there were more than ten fatal killings a year in each of several urban centers, including New York, Los Angeles, Chicago, and Detroit. The study examined fatal police shootings in relation to population size, rate of violent crime, rate of homicide, size of the police force, and rate of arrest for violent crime.

Though the findings from both government reports are interesting, they point to an empirical catch-22. The data are insufficient to sound an alarm regarding police killings. Thus, absent a national baseline, there is no definitive way to determine whether these incidents represent racially biased policing or something else. Without more statistics, it is unlikely that the problem of police brutality will result in national policy changes. Interestingly, such data are required by law. The Crime Control Act of 1994 directs the U.S. attorney general to collect and publish annual data on police shootings.

IV. "What Did I Do to Be So Black and Blue?"[18]

In encounters with the police, young Black men are often portrayed as fearless and bold. Media images, from the nightly news to rap music videos, often picture a swaggering, "devil-may-care" young Black man who is ready to take on the police or anyone else who crosses his path. For some young Black men, this representation is an accurate depiction; for many others, it is not. Either way, for many police officers, when they encounter young Black men, they see the tough-boy facade and act accordingly.

One concern about this representation is its impact on the interactions between Black men and the police. Young Black men have the highest probability of being stopped and, therefore, harassed by the police. This remains true whether they are driving while Black, walking while Black, running while Black, standing while Black, shopping while Black, sitting while Black, bicycling while Black, or breathing while Black (see chapter 6). The high rate of interaction between Blacks and the police is not new.

Historical records indicate the existence of longstanding tensions between police and African Americans. For example, there is a direct link between law enforcement and lynching.[19] In some instances, the records indicate that police officers participated in lynchings or acted as silent partners in White mob attacks against Blacks. This typically occurred in cases involving a Black man arrested on suspicion of sexual assault against a White woman.[20] Related to this, some of the contemporary, well-known incidents of police brutality (e.g., those involving Jonny Gammage, Tyisha Miller, Malice Green, and Amadou Diallo) have the markings of a lynching.

Given U.S. history, it is little wonder that, for many Blacks, police killings tap into long-held fears of unprovoked, random, and brutal attacks by law enforcement. These assaults are inexplicable except for the victim being of the wrong race, in the wrong place, at the wrong time. This lynching legacy partly explains the visceral, negative reaction many Blacks today have toward the police. Stories of encounters with "the law" in which a relative was left bruised, battered, or buried, have been passed down through generations like heirlooms. These stories are echoed in Black literature. One example is Langston Hughes's fictional character Jesse B. Simple, who declares, "I definitely do not like the Law."[21] The historically oppressive relationship between the police and the Black community is lost in contemporary discussions.

"Climate of Mutual Threat." According to conflict theory, social institutions operate to control state interests. Institutions such as the criminal

justice system are structured to control marginal groups (e.g., racial minorities) in society. These groups are most likely to experience an exercise of state control when they are perceived as threats to the dominant racial group. Specifically, the "threat" hypothesis predicts that actions by individuals and groups that challenge the interests of the powerful are likely to be labeled deviant or criminal.[22] It follows from this theory that members of threatening groups are more likely to be victimized by police violence than are members of other groups.

As noted earlier, minority groups do not pose a threat just to the interests that police protect. They pose a threat to the officers themselves. This reasoning underlies arguments that focus on how dangerous policing is and the disproportionate rate of minority crime. The focus on the high rates of Black offending suggests that the police have good reason to fear young Black men.

The fact that Blackness is perceived as a threat to Whites as a group and to police officers as a group has paved the way for policing strategies that target and sanction potential minority offenders. In turn, these strategies support police practices that treat Blacks as representatives of society's deviance. This creates a dynamic relationship in which many Blacks are suspicious and fearful of the police and many Whites and law enforcement officials are fearful of African Americans. Malcolm Holmes describes the resulting relationship as a "climate of mutual threat":[23]

> Minority citizens . . . distrust the police whom they view as threatening symbols of oppression. They may be more antagonistic to the police, which increases the severity of both formal and informal police sanctions against them. Minority antagonism also may precipitate extra-legal violence, including deadly force, against the police. The climate of mutual threat means that the mere presence and visibility of minorities may amplify the perception of risk among police officers.[24]

This climate of distrust has created a social and racial impasse within policing and in African American communities. It is fueled by what takes place after an incident of police brutality, discussed in the following section.

V. The "Roundabout" (a.k.a. the Police Brutality Dance)

A look at how police brutality cases typically unfold raises a single question: "What just happened?" This inquiry logically follows from the proceedings in police brutality cases. The process is a slightly more sophisti-
cated form of the magician's smoke-and-mirrors trick. In far too many instances, an allegation of police violence is met with a series of predictable,
you-can-set-your-watch-by-it, highly ritualized public responses. This is
the police brutality dance, or what is labeled the "roundabout." It is a lot
like most dances in that once you know the basic step, there is room for
individual variation. The roundabout has six basic steps:

- Step 1: There is an incident of alleged police violence against a person of color.
- Step 2: There are expressions of outrage by members of the minority community. This is followed by calls for calm by the authorities
  (e.g., mayor or chief of police).
- Step 3: The authorities publicly classify the incident as an "aberra-
  tion," emphasize that most police officers do a good job, and im-
  plore citizens not to rush to judgment.
- Step 4: There are attempts to portray the victim of the alleged police abuse as a "bad" victim (e.g., highlighting the victim's prior
  criminal record or the fact that the victim was engaged in deviant
  behavior at the time of the assault).
- Step 5: There are community protests (e.g., marches, rallies, and
  vigils) held in the victim's community. These, too, are met with
  calls for calm by the authorities. The mainstream press depicts the
  community organizers as opportunistic or as unfairly impugning
  the reputations of the police because of a few "bad apples." Comparable incidents of prior abuse (involving the same officers or
  precinct) are released.
- Step 6: A grand jury reviews the case and declines to issue a criminal indictment. The victim's family members and community organizers ask the U.S. attorney general to investigate the case.

The steps of the roundabout may vary according to the case. For example, in some instances the grand jury issues an indictment or the prosecutor decides not to file charges. In others, the defendant enters a plea. In
some instances, the FBI intervenes. Case-specific variations notwith-

standing, police assaults against minorities continue at a steady pace. Most problematic, the roundabout—like the cha-cha, the hustle, the macarena, and the electric slide—simply repeats itself. In fact, sometimes a new variation of the dance—another police assault against a person of color—begins before the prior routine has run its course. The roundabout, with its entrenched circularity, offers a paradoxical denouement— an ending that signifies a new beginning.

The roundabout underscores one of the key dynamics in current discussions of police abuse. At one end of the spectrum, there are those who argue that police brutality is a problem. Proponents of this view cite cases involving police officers who have been overzealous in their use of force. At the other end, there are those who argue that the police have a difficult job; rather than being criticized, they should be praised. Further, they argue, incidents of abusive policing are rare. The NYPD Benevolent Association's fall 2000 subway campaign exemplifies this position. The campaign posters read: "Most people wouldn't take this job for a million bucks, a New York City police officer does it for a lot less."[25] The picture accompanying the ad shows an officer lying dead in a pool of blood, killed in the line of duty. Not surprisingly, for these opposing sides, the twain never meets.

This standoff makes it difficult to have a productive discussion on how to handle the problem of police assault. The issue of excessive force is allowed to fester until it can no longer be ignored, rather than being addressed proactively. The findings of numerous police commissions (e.g., the Christopher, Mollen, and Ramparts commissions) offer notorious examples of the problem. Beyond representing an ineffective method of problem-solving, a reactive approach to police abuse further marginalizes those groups most likely to bear the brunt of excessive force practices.

One way that accountability can be addressed is to handle the problem of "blue rage," the term used by Sergeant Preston Gilstrap, of the National Black Police Association.[26] It describes situations in which police encounter a suspect whom they fear or who poses a physical threat to their safety. In these situations, police respond to the suspect on the basis of fear and are likely to use more force than is necessary to control the situation. Gilstrap suggests that something must be done to both temper and sanction this rage. As noted earlier, race ties directly to this issue. Black men are most likely to be viewed as criminal threats, and, therefore, they bear the brunt of this rage. It appears that holding the police accountable for abuse and brutality necessitates some assessment of the dimensions of blue rage. Otherwise, the roundabout will continue un-abated.

VI. Conclusion: Who Bears the Costs of a Free Society?

In recent years, there have been a handful of cases involving a police as-sault against a Black person. These incidents, however, obscure the more routine instances of police abuse, such as the use of traffic stops to harass and berate citizens or of antiloitering laws to target African American males.[27] These cases make up the majority of police-minority interac-tions. They also set the stage for the more egregious acts of police bru-tality.

Precious little attention—empirical, legal, political, or otherwise—is focused on the large-scale impact of this reality. What does it mean when a society ritually sacrifices the constitutional and civil rights of its racial minorities? Beyond the potential psychological consequences of such ac-tions, how does this reality influence the perception of Blacks by members of other racial groups? How does it shape how Blacks view themselves? How Blacks view Whites? It is unreasonable to expect that Blacks can and will shrug off this "go directly to jail; do not pass go" mentality. As Randall Kennedy asks, what about the danger that "threatens all Ameri-cans when cynicism and rage suffuse a substantial sector of the commu-nity"?[28]

Our hands-off approach to police brutality stands in stark contrast to the empathic treatment society usually reserves for innocent victims of crime. We have the same litany of responses to minority claims of police abuse that we have to our next-door neighbors' domestic dispute: Let's not get involved; We really don't know what happened; Let them work it out; There's probably a good explanation for their fight; We don't know all of the facts; and (the clincher) It's none of our business. Such ration-ales, when used to dismiss harm to an identifiable segment of the popu-lation, diminish the collective harm of police brutality. Police violence af-fects each of us, as individuals and as members of racial groups and of so-ciety at large.

Most of us have passively watched as police brutality has increasingly been framed as a Black issue. We have watched as variations of the round-about have been performed. We have observed incident after incident after incident of police abuse. In fact, the number of cases we have read about, heard about, and experienced is mind-numbing. The toll of these incidents has been so profound that it now takes an other-worldly police assault to rattle us. We are no longer shocked to learn that, in the hands of an African American, a candy wrapper, a key chain, a wallet, or a cell phone has been fatally mistaken for a gun. This contemporary reality ensures that next week, next month, and next year there will be another headline-grabbing police brutality case—one with different facts and a different victim's name.

5

Black Protectionism

I will never berate a fellow African American.
—C-SPAN caller in response to a press story about
Jesse Jackson's out-of-wedlock child (April 1, 2001)[1]

I. Introduction

A look at how African Americans treat high-profile members of its community who have been accused of criminal or unethical activity shows that the community is between a rock and hard place. On the one hand, African Americans as a group believe in the Puritan work ethic—play by the rules and you will succeed. On the other hand, as a group they are acutely aware that this ideology must be tempered by the harsh reality of American racism. This chapter offers a detailed analysis of how African Americans respond to community members who have fallen from grace. A review of two contemporary cases, O. J. Simpson and Clarence Thomas, begins the discussion.

Throughout the O. J. Simpson murder trial, polls indicated that African Americans overwhelmingly believed that he was not guilty. Following the verdict, Black support for Simpson reached 82 percent, compared with 38 percent White support (table 5-1). In 1991, after Clarence Thomas was nominated to the U.S. Supreme Court, African Americans

TABLE 5-1

O. J. Simpson: Support for Nonguilty Verdict by Race

	Approve	Disapprove	No Opinion
Blacks	82%	9%	9%
Whites	38%	54%	8%

Source: Gallup poll, October 19, 1995.

TABLE 5-2

Clarence Thomas: Support for Seat on the U.S. Supreme Court, by Race (1991)

	July–August 1991	September–October 1991*
Blacks	50%	68%
Whites	53%	52%

* Taken following Anita Hill's allegations of sexual harassment.

Source: Gallup poll, August–October 1991.

stood firmly behind him during his Senate confirmation hearings. Black support ranged from 50 percent to 68 percent in the period between his nomination and his Senate confirmation (table 5-2). The Black community's support for Thomas reached its zenith after he claimed he was the victim of a "high-tech lynching," which came on the heels of sexual assault allegations by Anita Hill, a former employee. Thomas's historical allusion to the thousands of Blacks killed at the hands of racist Whites, including mobs, Klansmen, and state officials, was undeniably powerful. For many Blacks, the all-White and all-male Senate Judiciary Committee represented an eerily familiar attempt to bring down another Black man.

Both the Simpson and the Thomas cases shed light on how crime and deviance by Blacks are labeled and represented, and on how the Black community has responded. Historically, many of these cases have involved sporting events. The aftermath of the 1910 heavyweight bout between a Black man, Jack Johnson, and his White opponent, Jim Jeffries, offers a dramatic example. Johnson beat Jeffries, whom many had dubbed the "great White hope," in a fifteen-round match and became the first Black heavyweight boxing champion. Johnson, who boasted of his pugilistic abilities and was often seen in the company of White women, was loathed by many Whites. Some were so angered by his defeat of Jeffries that riots erupted in cities across the country. More than a dozen Blacks were killed by White mobs, hundreds were seriously injured, and the police made thousands of arrests for disorderly conduct.

Numerous other Black athletes have had to carry the race mantle, their athletic prowess serving as a proxy for the humanity of the Black race. Examples include Joe Louis, Jackie Robinson, and Muhammad Ali. Today, the level of acceptance of Black athletes and entertainers is often used as a watermark indicating how race relations have advanced over time.

The term "Black protectionism"[2] describes the cloak of racial support that Blacks readily provide for condemned Black leaders and celebrities.

Although race-based group interest is not limited to Blacks, this chapter argues that the form of protectionism practiced by African Americans is unique. This chapter provides a detailed exploration of Black protectionism. The first section explores its theoretical bases—why it exists and the purposes it serves, including how it acts as a buffer against White racism. The second part outlines the operating mechanisms of Black protectionism. The third section analyzes specific applications of protectionism, who has received it and who has been denied it. The fourth section assesses the costs and benefits of Black protectionism. The discussion details the ways that protectionism operates as a shield against the coded message that Blackness can be equated with deviance.

II. Social Problems, Conspiracies, Shared History, and Shared Space: A Look at Theory

Labeling as a Social Problem. The literature on social problems offers a theoretical starting point for understanding Black protectionism. This research explores how groups come to define a condition as a problem and how they take steps to solve the problem.[3] Juvenile delinquency, high crime rates, and prison overcrowding are examples of social problems. One way of thinking about Black protectionism is to see it as the Black community's response to being labeled deviant. In other words, the Black community's reaction to being labeled a social problem has been to label that very labeling a social problem. The belief of many African Americans that they are viewed as a dysfunctional group is based upon many factors, including their experiences within the justice system. This perception is enhanced by myriad media portrayals of Blacks as dysfunctional; these images emphasize disproportionate rates of arrest, conviction, and imprisonment and a laundry list of other negative social indices, such as high rates of out-of-wedlock births, failure to complete high school, single-parent households, infant mortality, and unemployment.

In this view, the Black community's disproportionately high rate of social marginality is directly tied to America's history of racism. Black protectionism operates as a buffer to racial stereotyping and labeling. Thus, protectionism is a rational response to being labeled.

Conspiracies. The literature on conspiracies offers additional insight into the workings of Black protectionism. In fact, there is an empirical relationship between conspiracy theories and Black protectionism. For many Blacks, racist conspiracies against Blacks serve as tracking devices that locate and label White oppression. Patricia Turner's *I Heard It through the Grapevine*, reviews some of the many conspiracy theories operating within the Black community. One of the more commonly held beliefs is that there is a government plot to destroy the Black man. This view is evident in rumors that the government or large corporations have plans to poison, maim, or kill African Americans (e.g., through imported drugs or tainted foods). Turner identifies two kinds of drug-related conspiracies: malicious intent and benign neglect. The former involves the belief that there is a specific plan in operation. An example of a malicious-intent conspiracy is the belief that crack cocaine was intentionally planted in urban areas to decimate the Black community. Benign neglect conspiracies are those that do not require intent to harm; rather, the harm is caused by the government's failure to protect members of the African American community. Slow response times by the police who answer calls for service in Black neighborhoods and the failure to stop the influx of drugs into urban areas are examples of benign neglect conspiracies.

In one notable study, peer group sessions were held to empirically test the prevalence of Black conspiracy theories.[4] In this 1995 study, Theodore Sasson conducted small-group interviews with fifty-one adults (mostly Black). He found that conspiracies serve two key functions. First, they are used to make sense of disproportionately high rates of social dysfunction (e.g., arrest and conviction rates). Second, they promote in-group solidarity by reinforcing a shared historical narrative. As well, Sasson found that conspiracies are typically expressed in vague terms—the perceived conspirators are an interchangeable group of villains that includes the police, the media, and White society in general. Sasson concludes that because there is little room in the public discourse for acknowledging the impact of White racism on Black life, many Blacks perceive that there is a wide and vast array of potential conspirators.

Regina Austin's work underscores Sasson's findings. Her research indicates that anti-Black conspiracy theories have a functional purpose. They act as a critical response to the social and political marginialization of Blacks by mainstream institutions. She states:

> [Anti-Black conspiracies] circulate[e] through available channels not controlled by the dominant white society. . . . Through theorizing, blacks

express what they are concerned about in the way that is unmediated by the strictures of conventional reporting. . . . [T]he theories come close to being free, uncensored speech. There is a logic and a rationality to many anti-Black conspiracy theories. Although they sometimes have a fantastic quality, the theories offer explanations at a time when bad things are happening to blacks and no one is adequately explaining why.[5]

The creation of conspiracy theories is a predictable and useful instrument for historically oppressed racial groups.

Shared History and Shared Space. In addition to social problems and conspiracy theories, the shared history of African Americans, and the tightly bonded geographical community it has forged underlie, Black protectionism. This shared history includes slavery, lynching, and legally sanctioned segregation in all public accommodations. Further, state policies and practices, such as housing restrictions in the form of restrictive covenants, redlining, and racial steering, made it difficult for Blacks to improve their condition. Until the 1960s, the Federal Housing Administration financed homes in White suburban areas but provided virtually no mortgage insurance in urban markets, where most Blacks resided.

A contemporary look at residential housing patterns dramatically illustrates the impact of these race-based policies and practices. In *American Apartheid,* Douglas Massey and Nancy Denton use 1990 Census tract data to explore residential patterns by race. Their research indicates that African Americans are not only segregated; they are *hyper*segregated. Most Blacks live in racially isolated clusters, away from other racial groups.[6] These stark housing patterns were found in almost all major metropolitan centers, where more than 80 percent of Blacks live. These areas include Atlanta, Baltimore, Chicago, Detroit, Los Angeles, New York, and Philadelphia. A study based on the 2000 Census, conducted almost ten years later, reported similar findings.[7] Whites live in neighborhoods that are 80 percent White, and Blacks live in neighborhoods that are 75.5 percent Black. Cincinnati, Cleveland, Detroit, Miami, Newark, and New York are among the cities with the largest number of segregated neighborhoods.

The density and shape of the residential community has implications for the social community. For instance, it determines whether the social community will be a tightly knit one; people who live closer to one another are more likely to remain in close contact. Further, the relatively small size of the Black community (13 percent of the U.S. population) enhances its ability to remain close. Its shared history and space have helped to create a race-based community, one with its own identity. As a result, to some degree, individual identities have been muted. Thus, an attack on one member of the group, especially a successful, high-profile member, may be interpreted as an attack upon the group itself. When one member of the group is under the public microscope, as O. J. Simpson was, that person becomes a stand-in for the entire community of Black people. One contemporary manifestation of African Americans' shared history and shared space is a deep distrust of the criminal justice system in particular. The historical reality of an unjust legal system is combined with the contemporary reality of a system that produces, among other things, disproportionate arrests, sentences, and convictions of African Americans.

The research on social problems, conspiracies, and shared history and space situates Black protectionism within the empirical literature. The next section explores the mechanics of Black protectionism.

III. Operating Mechanisms and Potential Beneficiaries of Black Protectionism

Operating Mechanisms. Table 5-3 identifies the four operating mechanisms for Black protectionism. The first, an allegation of wrongdoing, can be established by either an allegation of criminal conduct or an allegation of unethical conduct. The second requirement is that the allegation of wrongdoing be made against someone Black. Here, the age-old "one-drop" rule applies. Even people who identify themselves as only partly Black (e.g., Tiger Woods) and those who are "colorless" (e.g., O. J. Simpson and Clarence Thomas) are eligible for Black protectionism.

TABLE 5-3

Operating Mechanisms for Black Protectionism

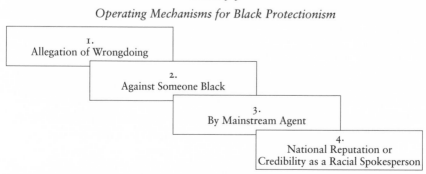

1.
Allegation of Wrongdoing

2.
Against Someone Black

3.
By Mainstream Agent

4.
National Reputation or
Credibility as a Racial Spokesperson

TABLE 5-4
Trigger Questions For Black Protectionism

Whites	Blacks
1. Did he commit the offense?	1. Did he commit the offense?
	2. Even if he did, was he set up?
	3. Would he risk everything he has (e.g., wealth, fame, material possessions) to commit an offense?
	4. Is he the only person who has committed the offense?
	5. Do Whites accused of committing the same offense receive the same scrutiny and treatment?
	6. Is this accusation part of a conspiracy to destroy the Black race?

Third, the allegation of wrongdoing must come from a mainstream agent outside the Black community. Examples include a government official or government body, such as a district attorney, congressional committee, or the police. Finally, the person alleged to have engaged in misconduct must be someone with national recognition or credibility as a racial spokesperson.[8] Those who can meet this four-part test include celebrities, politicians, athletes, and businessmen. The bottom line is that the targeted person must have something valuable to lose.

Table 5-4 contrasts the various questions that Blacks ask when analyzing an allegation against a well-known Black person and the single question that Whites ask. For Blacks, the answer to the first question, "Did he commit the offense?" is not determinative. Black protectionism may be granted whether the answer is yes or no. When the answer to the second question, "Is there is any indication that the person was set up?" is yes, Black protectionism may be triggered. The third question— "Would the person jeopardize his status by committing an offense?"—is more rhetorical than substantive. The answer is usually negative. The fourth and fifth questions call for a comparison between how Blacks and Whites are treated by society. If the answers to "Is he the only person who has committed the offense?" and "Do Whites accused of committing the same offense recieve the same scrutiny and treatment?" are "no," Black protectionism may be triggered. It is unlikely that there will be a definitive answer to the sixth question; thus, "maybe" is a sufficient response. If the answer is yes or maybe, Black protectionism may be applied. These six questions have consistently surfaced in discussions of the Black community's response to criminal and ethical allegations against Black leaders and celebrities.

These race-laden queries provide some insight on why Blacks are more likely to protect and defend members of their own racial group. Again, the history of racism against African Americans, which includes government-sanctioned plots to silence Black leadership, has created a deep-rooted skepticism of government actions. The next section considers the pool of potential recipients and the actual beneficiaries of Black protectionism.

Potential Recipients. Table 5-5 lists some of the potential recipients of Black protectionism. It primarily highlights cases from 1990 to 2002 and includes the alleged crime or unethical conduct. Many of these cases received national attention. The analysis of Black protectionism is limited to incidents involving well-known Blacks to facilitate an assessment of the larger Black community. Case information has been gathered from various sources, including national polls, national newspapers, and Black media.

Table 5-5 includes a broad list of African Americans (e.g., athletes, religious leaders, elected officials, entertainers, cabinet members, businessmen, and civil rights leaders). In most cases, the alleged criminal conduct involved white-collar crime, such as fraud, embezzlement, or bribery. Some cases involve violent crime, such as rape or murder. A small number involve what some would label victimless crimes, including drug use and gambling.

Beneficiaries. Table 5-6 lists the names of some African Americans who have benefited from Black protectionism and some who have not, and other difficult-to-classify cases. Where available, survey data were used to assess and measure the degree of support the person was given by the Black community. Where poll data indicated that more than one-half of the Blacks surveyed believed the person was innocent (or unfairly charged), Black protectionism was found to exist. In cases where more than 50 percent of the community adopted a particular perspective, the viewpoint was considered to cross economic class lines. A 50 percent rating means that Blacks from both the lower and middle classes were included. Further, a 50 percent threshold indicates that at least one-half of the Black community adopted a particular viewpoint. Through case-specific examples, the next section analyzes who is eligible for Black protectionism.

TABLE 5-5

Potential Recipients of Black Protectionism, 1990–2003

Name	Allegation
Marion Barry[a]	Drug Use
Ron Brown	Bribery
Kobe Bryant[b]	Sexual Assault
Rae Carruth	Murder
Rae Carruth	Murder
Ben Chavis	Fraud; extramarital affair with NAACP coworker
Sean "P. Diddy" Combs	Illegal possession of a firearm; bribery; assault
Joycelyn Elders	Inappropriate remarks
Mike Espy	Bribery
Lani Guinier	Inappropriate writings
Alcee Hastings[a]	Bribery
Alexis Herman	Bribery
Jesse Jackson	Extramarital affair; embezzlement
Michael Jackson	Child sexual assault
R. Kelly	Sex with minor; child pornography
Ray Lewis	Murder
Henry Lyons	Extramarital affair; embezzlement
Carol Mosely-Brown	Mismanagement of funds
Hazel O'Leary	Excessive spending; mismanagement of funds
Melvin Reynolds	Extramartial affair; sex with minor; child pornography; phone sex
Carl Rowan	Unlawful possession of a firearm
O. J. Simpson	Murder
Clarence Thomas	Sexual harassment
Mike Tyson	Rape; aggravated assault
Chris Webber	Speeding; marijuana possession; gambling
Jayson Williams	Involuntary manslaughter

[a] pre-1990

[b] August 2003 poll data indicated a racial divide—more Blacks believe Bryant is innocent

IV. *Patterns and Practices*

Political Officials

Historically, the African American community has revered its political leadership, particularly its elected representatives. This reverence is partly a testament to the historical and contemporary roadblocks placed in the path of would-be Black politicians and voters. For example, today, national-level Black politicians face particular challenges.[9] Studies consistently indicate that Whites are reluctant to vote for Black politicians. Since 1965, when the Voting Rights Act was passed, Douglass Wilder has been the only African American elected governor, and Carol Moseley-Braun and Edward Brooke the only elected Black senators. At the local level, however, there have been increases in the number of Black elected officials. This section looks at how the Black community has responded to allegations made against some Black political leaders. The case of Adam Clayton Powell offers a history lesson and acts as a starting point for this discussion.

Adam Clayton Powell. With their entry into electoral politics, Blacks faced intense scrutiny and abuse.[10] This scrutiny has historical roots. In 1944, Adam Clayton Powell was elected as the congressional representative for Harlem. A few years into his term, he came under attack because he did not support Adlai Stevenson, who was heading the Democrats' presidential ticket. Stevenson had minimized the importance of a civil rights amendment and refused to meet with Powell and other congressmen to discuss his position. In 1953, following the election of Dwight Eisenhower as president, Powell was charged with tax evasion. The government's three-thousand-dollar evasion claim against Powell cost more than $100,000 to prosecute. Following his embrace of the Black Power movement, Powell was removed from Congress in 1967 by a vote of 364-64. Powell's case went before the U.S. Supreme Court, which decided that he had been wrongly removed. Powell ran again for office but lost to another Black politician, Charles Rangel.

TABLE 5-6

Whether Black Protectionism Applies, Select Cases

Yes	No
Marion Barry	Rae Carruth
[Bill Clinton]	Joycelyn Elders
Jesse Jackson	Lani Guinier
R. Kelly	Alexis Herman
Melvin Reynolds	Chris Webber
O. J. Simpson	Jayson Williams
Clarence Thomas	
Mike Tyson	

The Powell case provides a dramatic illustration of the difficulties faced by some Black politicians. The government has engaged in an intense and prolonged surveillance of progressive, and radical politicians and organizations, including the Black Panther Party.[11] This reality partly explains the strong support that Black politicians receive from the Black community. With this history in mind, it is not surprising that Black politicians have been granted Black protectionism.

Jesse Jackson. The Reverend Jesse Jackson has been an active civil rights leader for more than four decades. He has held a variety of posts, including a brief term as shadow senator in the District of Columbia. His other roles include peacekeeper, presidential adviser, hostage negotiator, corporate diversity broker, boycott leader, and head of Rainbow PUSH and the Citizenship Education Fund (CEF). In January 2001, Jackson, who is the married father of five, admitted fathering a child with a mistress.[12] The story, which first appeared in the *National Enquirer,* was widely reported by the tabloids and the mainstream press. The mother of Jackson's two-year-old love child, Karin Stanford, had been a Rainbow PUSH consultant and had authored a biography of Jackson.

These stories triggered intense media interest. Jackson held press conferences to respond to the charges. Because of information that was subsequently released, the CEF's financial management became an issue. As well, Stanford's receipt of forty thousand dollars to relocate from Washington, D.C., to California was criticized. During this period, Jackson maintained a high profile within the Black community, including a well-timed, very late arrival at a nationally televised panel on the state of Black America, hosted by Tavis Smiley. The crowd gave him a rousing, minutes-long, standing ovation. Polls indicated that support for Jackson remained strong within the Black community.[13] This allegiance may be partly attributable to the timing of the press reports. On January 20, 2001, Jackson was scheduled to lead a national rally in Tallahassee, Florida. The march was designed to draw attention to the 2000 Florida election scandal and to protest the presidential inauguration of George W. Bush. Two days before the scheduled forum, the Jackson story broke.

Marion Barry. The case involving former Washington, D.C., mayor Marion Barry offers an interesting application of Black protectionism. In January 1990, Barry was captured on videotape in a D.C. hotel room with a woman who was not his wife, smoking a crack pipe. The FBI had used Barry's former girlfriend, Hazel Diane "Rasheeda" Moore, to lure him to the hotel suite. Moore, who had agreed to participate in the sting, was paid $1,700 a month by the FBI. The two-hour videotape indicates that Barry was as interested in having sex as he was in using drugs. The fact that Barry's criminal conduct was captured on videotape sets this case apart from others: There is no dispute that Barry actually engaged in criminal activity. In a split jury verdict, Barry was convicted of drug possession and acquitted of all other charges.

As the trigger questions in table 5-4 indicate, the racial target's guilt or innocence is not decisive in assessing whether Black protectionism applies. This is evident in the Black community's response to Barry's arrest and prosecution. Many Blacks opined that the mayor had gone to Moore's room for a sexual liaison, not to smoke crack cocaine. The central focus in Barry's case was not the first trigger question but the second and the sixth queries. Thus, the inquiry shifted from "Did he commit the offense?" to "Even if he did, was he set up?" and "Is this accusation part of a conspiracy to destroy the Black race?" The Barry case suggests that Black protectionism operates to mitigate charges that Blacks view as overreaching by the state.

Melvin Reynolds. In 1995, Representative Mel Reynolds, of Illinois, was charged with having sex with Beverly Heard, a minor. The sixteen-year-old Heard was a campaign volunteer. At that time, Reynolds was already under investigation for election campaign violations. Though Reynolds denied any physical contact with Heard, he admitted to engaging her in "phone sex." The following year, a jury convicted the married congressman of criminal sexual assault, child pornography, obstruction of justice, and aggravated criminal sexual abuse. In 1997, Reynolds, a Rhodes scholar, was sentenced to six and one-half years in federal prison.

The reaction in this case mirrored, to a lesser degree, that in the Barry incident. Very few sought to justify Reynolds's actions. The focus shifted away from Reynolds's involvement (first trigger question) to both the *actions* of the federal prosecutor's office against him and the *inactions* of the federal prosecutor's office against other (non-Black) elected officials (fifth trigger question). For example, some described the prosecutors as overzealous in his case. Others offered the case of Senator Bob Packwood, of Oregon, as proof that Reynolds was being held to a different,

more punitive standard. Packwood had been accused of sexually assaulting more than two dozen female staffers during his congressional tenure.
He resigned and faced no criminal charges.

Bill Clinton: The First Black President. Arguably the most provocative
and controversial recipient of Black protectionism has been former president Bill Clinton. Within the Black community, Clinton has in many
ways been viewed and treated as an African American. Social commentators, from Nobel laureate Toni Morrison to comedian Chris Rock, have
referenced Clinton's "Black" skin.[14] In 1998, Morrison detailed the
racialized treatment Clinton received by the mainstream press:

> White skin notwithstanding, this is our first Black president. Blacker
> than any actual person who could be elected in our children's lifetime
> . . . Clinton displays almost every trope of Blackness: single-parent
> household, born poor, working-class, saxophone-playing, McDonald's-
> and junk-food-loving boy from Arkansas.[15]

In addition to fitting these stereotypes, Clinton also had a Black best
friend and appeared genuinely comfortable around working-class Black
people. All of this set him apart from other presidents and from White
politicians in general. As an honorary Black person, Clinton received
Black protectionism's highest vote count. Following the allegations and
admissions that the married president had had sexual relations with a
twenty-four-year-old White House intern, poll data indicated that the
overwhelming majority of Blacks stood behind him. His approval ratings
peaked during his impeachment. In fact, the Black voting bloc consistently represented one of Clinton's strongest bases of support.

This Black well of support was again on display following Clinton's
departure from the White House. After he faced heated criticism about
his first choice in office space—a midtown Manhattan office that rented
for almost $1 million annually—Clinton opted to move uptown, to
Harlem. On the heels of this, his granting of an executive pardon and
clemency in several controversial cases was heavily criticized. As before,
his Black support base remained steadfast. In a further twist, in October
2002, Clinton was inducted into the Arkansas Black Hall of Fame. Clinton was its first and only White inductee.[16]

In an unpredictable union of these three men, Reynolds, who served
three years of his sentence, was released in 2000, following a grant of

clemency by Bill Clinton. Jesse Jackson's Rainbow PUSH organization subsequently hired him as a consultant on prison reform.

Black Women

Only a handful of Black women have been eligible for Black protectionism. Of these, none have received it. This raises the question of whether Black protectionism is available to Black women. The fact that few Black women have been eligible for its protection may simply mirror national trends, which indicate that women have relatively low rates of involvement in the criminal justice system. What follows is a discussion of four Black women who could have benefitted from Black protectionism: Carol Moseley-Braun, Alexis Herman, Lani Guinier, and Joycelyn Elders.

Carol Moseley-Braun. In 1992, Moseley-Braun became the first elected Black female senator. During her tenure, she faced allegations that she had used campaign funds for personal expenses, ignored claims that her campaign manager and then-fiancé had sexually harassed staff members, and maintained an alliance with a controversial Nigerian leader. Ultimately, there was no finding of criminal wrongdoing against Moseley-Braun. Ironically, Moseley-Braun, elected in the aftermath of the Clarence Thomas hearings, did not benefit from the same protectionism he had received. In 1998 she lost her re-election bid, in 1999 she was appointed U.S. ambassador to Samoa and New Zealand, and in 2003 she declared her candidacy for U.S. president in the 2004 election.

Alexis Herman. In 1998, Alexis Herman, secretary of labor under Clinton, faced allegations of bribery. Specifically, she was accused of having accepted $250,000 in illegal campaign contributions. A special prosecutor was appointed, and, after a two-year investigation, Herman was cleared of all charges. As was the case for Moseley-Braun, the Black community appeared to take little note of these charges—not enough to cause pollsters to track their reaction.

Lani Guinier and Joycelyn Elders. The incidents involving Lani Guinier and Joycelyn Elders are different from those involving Moseley-Braun and Herman. Neither case involved a charge of criminal or unethical conduct. These cases are noteworthy, however, because, at the time of the charges, both women were in high-profile posts and were accused of wrongdoing.

In 1993, Bill Clinton nominated Guinier to head the civil rights division of the U.S. attorney general's office. Conservatives rallied to oppose her nomination. Guinier, then a University of Pennsylvania law professor, was portrayed as a left-wing kook—a quota queen with "a strange name, strange hair, strange writings."[17] The day before Guinier's confirmation hearing was to begin, Clinton withdrew her name. He said that he had, only the night before, reviewed her legal scholarship and could not support her nomination. There was very little response from the Black community. Perhaps because the controversy involved arcane legal writing and because Guinier was accused not of a crime but rather "inappropriate" writings, support for her was less than forthcoming. Guinier, who now teaches at Harvard, is the first woman of color to receive tenure at the law school.

Similarly, Joycelyn Elders's forced resignation from her post as U.S. surgeon general did little to trigger Black interest or response. Elders served as surgeon general from 1993 to 1994. During her tenure, she made several frank remarks indicating her support for needle exchange programs, equal access to abortion, and the legalization of drugs. It was Elders's comments on sex education in grade school, however, that resulted in her dismissal. In response to a psychologist's question about whether she would promote masturbation to discourage school children from riskier forms of sexual activity, she stated, "I think that it is something that is a part of human sexuality and a part of something that perhaps should be taught."[18] A few days later, Clinton asked for Elders's resignation.

As noted, there was relatively little public comment on the cases involving Moseley-Braun, Herman, Guinier, or Elders. This is especially noteworthy in Herman's case, since she was charged with serious criminal conduct. Also, it is ironic that Elders received little vocal support from the African American community, considering that the focus of her work was on reducing the Black community's high rates of sexually transmitted diseases, particularly HIV/AIDS. Though neither Guinier's nor Elders's case involved a charge of misconduct—a common trigger for Black protectionism—both cases fell below the Black community's radar. In fact, there is no national poll information on the general public's reaction to any of these controversies. The muted community response to these four may be explained by the fact that each case involved a political scandal. Americans, not just African Americans, have demonstrated neither interest in nor surprise at low-level political scandals.

There is another possible interpretation of the Black community's lack of reaction to these women compared with its response to Jackson, Barry, Reynolds, and Clinton. It may be that, in order to earn the cloak of Black protectionism, you must pay your "race dues." Viewed alongside Jackson, Barry, Reynolds, and Clinton, Moseley-Braun, Herman, Guinier, and Elders, at the time they faced allegations of misconduct, had comparatively little name recognition. More to the point, they were not widely known as civil rights leaders. Though Guinier has a long history of legal activism in the struggle for civil rights, her work was not well known outside legal circles. To test this "race dues" hypothesis, there would need to be a case involving a Black woman whose civil rights track record was known and respected, someone such as civil rights veteran and congresswoman Maxine Waters.[19] The Black community's response to a criminal charge against Waters would be an ideal test of the role of gender in the working of Black protectionism. If Black protectionism did not extend to someone such as Waters, sexism would be a plausible explanation and a limitation of Black protectionism.

Regarding Guinier and Elders, it is also possible that their cases involved a test of competing allegiances. Clinton, who, arguably, is viewed as an honorary Black by many African Americans, was the person responsible for Guinier's withdrawal and Elders's resignation. It may be that, when forced to choose, Blacks extend protectionism to the person perceived to have the most racial seniority or recognition.

Cases Involving Sexual Assault

Mike Tyson and Desiree Washington. In 1992, Mike Tyson was charged with sexually assaulting Desiree Washington, a nineteen-year-old college student. Tyson met Washington during rehearsals for a beauty pageant. Washington was a contestant, Tyson a judge. Tyson called her later that evening, and they agreed to meet. At 1:30 A.M., Washington went to Tyson's hotel room, where, according to Washington, he raped her. Tyson was charged with and convicted of rape, and he served three years in prison.

Throughout the case, the Black community roundly denounced Washington. She was either blamed for her extreme naïveté (what, besides sex, would a grown man want from a woman in the middle of the night?) or labeled a scheming golddigger who planned to lure the boxing champ into a sexual encounter, have sex, "cry rape," then cash in.[20] Washington's assertion that she had no ulterior motives, that she was thrilled to meet Tyson, who was one of her father's sports heroes, fell on deaf ears.

As the trigger questions predict, many Blacks considered whether Tyson faced a double standard. During the same period that Tyson faced rape charges, William Kennedy Smith was acquitted of rape. Smith, the nephew of President John F. Kennedy, to-the-manor-born, and White, stood in stark contrast to Tyson, who had no elite pedigree, was Black, and was convicted of rape. The din of support for Tyson within the Black community all but drowned out voices of dissent; for example, following a "welcome home" parade for Tyson after his release from prison, several Black community activists staged a counterprotest.[21]

Clarence Thomas and Anita Hill. In July 1991, President George H. W. Bush nominated Clarence Thomas to fill the vacancy on the U.S. Supreme Court created by Justice Thurgood Marshall's retirement. Questions were raised within the civil rights and the Black communities as to whether Thomas was a worthy choice to succeed Marshall, the first African American Supreme Court Justice. Neither the NAACP nor the Urban League, however, publicly objected to Thomas's nomination. After being nominated, Thomas received lukewarm support. In September 1991, the press learned of Anita Hill's disclosures to the FBI. The Bureau had conducted a background check on Thomas. Hill, who had worked for Thomas twelve years earlier, alleged that he had routinely subjected her to crude, sexually explicit remarks and lewd behaviors.

In the wake of these allegations, the Black community's support for Thomas rose by more than ten percentage points.[22] Hill was portrayed as a scorned woman, as a woman in search of her fifteen minutes of fame on the back of a Black man, as a wild-eyed feminist suffering from delusional sexual fantasies ("erotomania"), and as a Black woman who was angry that her ex-lover, Thomas, had chosen to marry a White woman. Notably, however, none of this was established as fact. In October 1991, Thomas was confirmed by the Senate in a 52-48 vote.

In both the Tyson and Thomas cases, the Black woman was not as well known as the Black man. Until the allegations surfaced, most people had heard of neither Desiree Washington nor Anita Hill. Thus, neither Washington nor Hill had a "national reputation or credibility as a racial spokesperson" (table 5-3). It is notable, however, that Thomas was also not well known at the time he was nominated to the Supreme Court. By the time Hill's allegations surfaced, however, Thomas had a "national reputation" sufficient to trigger Black protectionism. It appears that whoever gets Black protectionism first "wins." Thus, Thomas was the first to stake a claim to the Black community's loyalty; even if it had wanted to support Hill, the community was already committed to Thomas.

A second, more complicated issue raised by the Tyson and Thomas cases is whether race trumps gender. More to the point, a strong case can be made that, within the Black community, issues of gender take a back seat to issues of race.[23] For example, when a Black man faces allegations of wrongdoing, within-race gender issues are dismissed as trifling inside skirmishes. Neither of these cases offers a complete test of the effect of gender on Black protectionism. It remains to be seen how the Black community would respond to a case in which a Black man accused a famous Black woman of criminal conduct, or one in which a famous Black woman accused a Black man of criminal conduct.

R. Kelly. The child pornography case involving the rhythm-and-blues crooner R. Kelly raises some interesting issues about the application of Black protectionism. In 2002, Kelly faced a twenty-one-count criminal indictment. One of the allegations was second-degree rape—specifically, engaging in sexual intercourse with a fourteen-year-old girl. Kelly, a married, thirty-three-year-old father of three, denied all charges. The crown jewel of the prosecution's case was a thirty-minute videotape of the alleged unlawful sexual activity. Underground copies of the video were sold on the street and circulated over the Internet. In response to the charges, Kelly released the song "Heaven I Need a Hug." The song includes the lyrics: "I gave thirteen years of my life to this industry / Hit song or not, I've given all of me / You smile in my face and tell me you love me / But then before you know the truth / You're so quick to judge me / Heaven I need a hug."[24]

Two aspects of the Kelly case deserve mention. First, there was a videotape. In this way, the case is comparable to the Barry case. Relative to Barry, Kelly recieved far less vocal support from African Americans.[25] There appeared to be a split in the Black community as to whether Kelly's personal issues should affect his career. What explains the apparently less than full cloak of protectionism? First, in Barry's case, many concluded that the government had overreached in its attempt to bring him down. By contrast, in Kelly's case, there was no evidence or speculation that the government was "out to get him." Second, it is likely that the crimes involved are viewed in very different lights. Many people might dismiss drug use as a "victimless" crime. However, they are likely to view sex between an adult and a minor as not only illegal but as immoral.

Third, unlike Barry and others who have benefited from Black protectionism, Kelly does not have a public reservoir of good will. It is likely that what little the public knew about his personal life did not work in his favor. When he was twenty-five, he married the then-fifteen-year-old singer Aaliyah. Also, throughout his career, Kelly has faced allegations that he has engaged in sex with underage girls, and his lust-laden lyrics themselves lend tacit support to the sex-related charges. However, in what could be viewed as a vote of confidence, Kelly's 2003 CD "Chocolate Factory" deubted at number one on the Billboard chart.

Political Stripes and "Good Acts." As table 5-6 indicates, the beneficiaries of Black protectionism represent a broad political continuum. Most, however, have been from the civil rights community. It is apparent that the cloak of Black protectionism is largely reserved for those who serve the Black community. The performance of "good acts," such as raising money to keep a local hospital open in a poor section of town or opening a day-care center for homeless children, may buffer any "bad acts." Marion Barry, Jesse Jackson, Mel Reynolds (table 5-6) have each promoted an explicitly pro-Black agenda. Each has performed what could be labeled good acts within the African American community.

The list of protectionism beneficiaries demonstrates, however, that there is no "pro-Black" litmus test for Black protectionism. If there were, neither Clarence Thomas (a self-proclaimed conservative Republican) nor O. J. Simpson (who considered himself "colorless" prior to the murder charges) would have received its protection.[26] As it stands, Black protectionism appears to be available to Black men without regard to political affiliation.

Rappers and Athletes—a Note. More than a few rappers have faced criminal charges. This gives rise to the question of whether they are eligible for Black protectionism. It appears that most rappers who have been charged with criminal offending do not meet the minimum requirements for Black protectionism. First, very few have achieved national recognition—a requirement for Black protectionism. Second, for various reasons, it appears that many people have low expectations for rappers. More to the point, the public is not surprised when they get into legal trouble. (See chapter 3 for a detailed discussion of the relationship between gangsta rap music and crime.) The Black community as a whole appears less concerned when a rapper is charged with criminal conduct than when other celebrity members of its community are accused of criminal conduct, although some segments within the Black community, notably young fans of hip-hop music, are likely to rally behind and support rappers charged with crime.

The same low expectations may also exist for young Black athletes. This may explain the muted response to homicide cases involving Rae Carruth, formerly with the NFL's Carolina Panthers, the NFL star Ray Lewis, of the Baltimore Ravens, and Jayson Williams, formerly a star player for the New Jersey Nets.[27] In these cases, there was no knee-jerk Black protectionism; instead, the community took a wait-and-see position.

This section has analyzed the dynamic nature of Black protectionism. The cases indicate that protectionism is partially triggered by how Whites and the mainstream media treat a fallen Black figure. For example, with Clarence Thomas, the all-White Senate Judiciary committee served as the catalyst for Black protectionism. Likewise, in the Simpson case, the perceived media bias against Simpson appears to have strengthened the cloak of Black protectionism.

V. Transformative, Mobilizing, or Simply Reactive? Costs and Benefits of Black Protectionism

This chapter has detailed the theories behind and the workings of Black protectionism. What is left to assess is the value of this practice, specifically, its costs and its benefits. An analysis of these questions allows for a determination of whether Black protectionism is transformative, mobilizing, or simply reactive.

Benefits of Black Protectionism

There are two interrelated benefits of Black protectionism. First, it reinforces group solidarity. When applied, it provides a common ground upon which Blacks can stand. Considering the political and economic diversity of the Black community, Black protectionism allows for a show of group strength and unity at a time when the group is increasingly viewed as politically and socially marginal.

Second, it operates as a sociopolitical statement. It says that, while conditions may have improved for Blacks, they have not improved *that* much. Specifically, Black protectionism serves as a reminder that historical forms of racial discrimination (e.g., slavery, slave codes, lynching, Black codes, and Jim Crow segregation) have contemporary manifestations. As well, Black protectionism operates as a link between past racial injustices and present racial abuses, such as racial profiling and police brutality. Thus, it acts as a counternarrative to mainstream assessments of racial progress. At a time when the Black community is routinely and rhetorically asked whether race relations are better today than they were forty years ago, Black protectionism operates as a history lesson. Opportunities for a general, public discussion of this history are few and far between.

Black protectionism allows African Americans to weigh and balance several factors before determining whether to provide support to a fallen leader. For instance, the community can compare the cost of an individual's moral lapse (e.g., adultery) with the benefit of an individual's "good acts" or other actions that benefit the community. The community can also make a distinction between what someone does in his public life and what someone does in his private life. Perhaps this cost-benefit approach is the result of the small number of Black politicians and celebrities. Black protectionism offers a way to resurrect those African Americans who get into trouble; it allows the Black elite to maintain its exalted status within the community.

Regina Austin observes that whether the Black community defends those who break the law depends upon considerations that others outside the community may not take into account. The Black community "evaluates behavior in terms of its impact on the overall progress of the race. Black criminals are pitied, praised, protected, emulated, or embraced if their behavior has a positive impact on the social, political, and economic well-being of black communal life."[28]

The benefits of Black protectionism operate as both an internal force within the Black community, fostering group solidarity, and an external force, sending a message to outsiders. It acts as a race relations barometer, an index of where the Black community and the White community are on issues of race and racism. For example, the need for Black protectionism reinforces itself each time a case arises and the White mainstream is perceived as being overzealous in its reaction to a case (e.g., the O. J. Simpson case) or as applying a guilty-until-proven-innocent analysis (e.g., the Marion Barry case).

Costs of Black Protectionism

The value of Black protectionism is obvious. It is a beneficial exercise of racial group solidarity. Questions remain, however, as to how it is applied and whether it carries some costs, as well.

Evidence of Wrongdoing. It appears that Black protectionism is granted regardless of culpability. Even in those cases where it is undisputed that the person accused of wrongdoing did engage in misconduct, Black protectionism may still operate. The Jesse Jackson and Marion Barry incidents are cases in point. When allegations surfaced that Jackson had fathered a child with his mistress, he issued a straightforward acknowledgment of paternity. In Barry's case, his drug use was captured on videotape and authenticated by his reaction after the police stormed his hotel room: "[The] bitch set me up."[29] Arguably, one of the costs of Black protectionism is its failure to differentiate between those who have engaged in misconduct and those who have not. This is a cost because some people outside the community may view it as a double standard and may be less likely to believe Black claims of racial bias, dismissing them as "crying wolf." Overlooking culpability is problematic, especially when there is no reprimand attached to Black protectionism.

No Reprimand, No Sanction. Interestingly, in instances where the allegations that prompt Black protectionism prove true, the Black community does not seek to impose any sanction against the person who benefits from Black protectionism. In reference to the phenomenon of embracing fallen heroes, Jill Nelson refers to African Americans as the "forgiving tribe."[30] There are several possible explanations for this. First, for some African Americans, the harsh actions of government officials, such as police officers or prosecutors, mitigate or excuse the accused person's offense. Second, there is a strong belief that what a person does in his private life should not be used to evaluate his professional capabilities. This viewpoint was evident during the Marion Barry, Bill Clinton, and Jesse Jackson scandals. Third, for some, being publicly shamed and being processed through the justice system is sanction enough.[31] As well, for many Blacks, any judgment, reprimand, or sanction should be left to a higher power. Fourth, some people believe that once one achieves certain material wealth and status, one is no longer held to the same standard as everyone else. Though such sentiment is rarely expressed openly, it appears to be a logical deduction based upon the high threshold that must be met before rich and famous Blacks are held accountable by the Black community. African Americans, of course, are not the only group to judge its rich and famous by a different standard.

Apolitical Black Protectionism. The race of the potential beneficiary appears to be the most important factor in determining whether Black protectionism will apply. African Americans across the political spectrum have benefited from protectionism. This apolitical application of Black protectionism raises an important question: Is it beneficial to the Black community to rally behind someone who does not adopt a mainstream civil rights agenda? How, for example, did the Black community benefit from its support of Clarence Thomas or O. J. Simpson?[32] It could be argued that in both cases Black protectionism did more harm than good. In his first decade on the U.S. Supreme Court, Thomas consistently voted against laws that protected Blacks' hard-won civil rights and liberties.[33] A review of his prenomination political affiliations and alliances, including his mentor, the now-retired conservative congressman John Danforth, and of his voting record as a federal judge accurately predicted his voting behavior on the Supreme Court. Many Blacks were either not aware of Thomas's political history or surmised that, once on the bench, he would "remember where he came from."

Likewise, the communal embrace of O. J. Simpson yielded little tangible benefit to African Americans. In fact, some have suggested that Black support for Simpson came at a high political price. Both cases demonstrate that knee-jerk protectionism, which may have short-term benefits, has long-term costs.

Blind Loyalty. The African American community's response to Bill Clinton offers a template for assessing whether Black protectionism at times works against Black interests. A detailed critique of Clinton's record on race and the justice system reveals some startling findings. Most notably, it was during Clinton's presidency that the nation's most punitive crime bill was signed into law.[34] In *The Debt*, Randall Robinson offers a critical analysis of the Black community's embrace of Bill Clinton. Robinson describes the community's apparent need to embrace leaders who appear outwardly friendly toward Blacks but who do not have the community's best interests at heart:

> No segment of the national electorate has given more but demanded and received less from the Democratic Party nationally than African Americans. We [Blacks] don't take ourselves seriously, therefore no one else does. Our support can be won with gestures.[35]

After highlighting some of Clinton's accomplishments, including a harsh welfare reform bill, Robinson concludes that Blacks are satisfied with symbolic gestures. Accordingly, Clinton was able to tap into the Black well of support largely by having high visibility in Black churches, having Black friends, taking trips to Africa, and appointing a race relations panel.[36] A closer evaluation of Clinton's actions on crime and race argue for a more informed application of Black protectionism.

The Black Monolith. Another potential cost of Black protectionism is that it presents the African American community as a monolith—one body, one voice. The idea of the Black monolith raises two interrelated concerns. First, it perpetuates a false reality. In truth, there are diverse viewpoints within the African American community. The sweep of Black protectionism casts aside alternate viewpoints. In large part, this is done because the media reads the support of a large number as representative of the entire group. For example, in the Simpson case, the 70 percent of Blacks who believed Simpson was innocent were allowed to represent 100 percent of the Black community.[37] Second, within the Black community, protectionism not only masks alternative viewpoints but discourages them. Little room is left for dissenters, who are perceived as airing dirty laundry. In fact, protectionism and the way it is portrayed by the mainstream press, may encourage group-based perspectives.

VI. Conclusion

This chapter argues that Black protectionism is an important, theoretically distinct, and empirically viable phenomenon. Black protectionism operates to guard against outside racial influences that affect the viability of leadership and status within the Black community. Most important, it acts as a counternarrative to centuries-old stereotypes of Black deviance. It took root during slavery, a time when a false or minor allegation against one African American could result in death or great bodily harm to scores of other African Americans. This history explains how it is that Black protectionism—akin to a confidence vote—applies without regard to political affiliation. Questions remain, however, about whether or when protectionism would operate to shield Black women and whether it is applied by Blacks to all those deemed worthy, regardless of their economic status. Future research will determine whether the current form of Black protectionism, which in some cases reflects a nuanced and thoughtful response by the Black community, is in the community's long-term best interests.

6

In the Crosshairs
Racial Profiling and Living while Black

I. Introduction

A Madison Avenue advertising agency could not have done a better job of putting racial profiling on the public map. In the early to mid-1990s, there were several prominent news stories involving Black men—rich and famous—who reported being stopped by the police because of their race.[1] The unstated text in these stories was that their high-profile status should serve as a proxy for their innocence. During this same period, there was a sharp rise in the prison population, and the percent of young Black men within the criminal justice system increased from one-quarter to one-third. In 1997, on the heels of these mounting stories and of a major U.S. Supreme Court decision in *Whren v. U.S.*,[2] Congressman John Conyers introduced the Traffic Stops Statistics Study Act. The bill was designed to provide a national gauge of the incidence and prevalence of racial profiling by police officers. Though neither the 1997 bill nor its 2000 version passed, the two proposals created a flurry of state-level legislative activity—a legislative jamboree. Dozens of states and police departments considered legislation that would mandate data collection by police during traffic stops. In 2001, the "End Racial Profiling Act" was introduced to Congress. The bill would allow an individual who has been harmed by racial profiling to file a civil lawsuit.

The speed with which racial profiling captured public attention is partly a response to how it has been labeled. The press quickly replaced "racial profiling" with a catchier expression, "Driving while Black."[3] In turn, this has been shortened to "DWB." Racial targeting has been a frequent topic of news and commentary, in print, television, and internet mediums. The practice has been denounced by Democrats and Republicans. Notably, presidents Bill Clinton and George W. Bush have both voiced opposition to racial profiling. In the academic arena, race-based stops, already the focus of constitutional and criminal procedure scholarship, have received increased interest and research attention. An array of legal, political, economic, and cultural entities have taken up the issue, from the American Bar Association to rap music luminaries. Some believe the issue has received more than its fifteen minutes of fame, while others believe the front-burner discussion is long overdue.

This chapter addresses several of the issues raised by racial profiling. The central thesis is that profiling offers another example of the myriad ways that Black skin and deviance continue to be linked—operating as an underground code. As is true for police brutality, racial profiling is not viewed as a general public threat; it is coded as a Black problem (for a discussion of police brutality, see chapter 4). The discussion includes a consideration of how profiling is defined and how these varied definitions have affected public discussions on the topic; a look at the legislative and legal responses designed to measure and stem racial profiling; an overview of the empirical research on profiling; examples of how Blackness has been equated with criminality; a review of the ways in which negative perceptions of Blackness are perpetuated through empirical research; and an analysis of the unintended consequences of failing to address the problems of racial profiling. The conclusion considers the future implications of profiling and provides suggestions for future empirical study.

II. Defining Terms

It seems that everyone has an opinion on what constitutes racial profiling. In fact, there is no uniform definition available in criminal justice textbooks, legal cases, or police procedure manuals. The term has been used to describe a wide range of activity. Three of the more common uses are presented here.

The Kitchen Sink—Generic Use. In some instances "racial profiling" is used to describe any action, by an individual or institution, that singles out minorities for unfavorable, discriminatory treatment; examples include store clerks who shadow Black patrons, police officers who target minority motorists, and transportation companies that eliminate or reduce routes to Black sections of town. Thus, any action that results in the heightened racial scrutiny of minorities—justified or not—constitutes racial profiling. Such an all-encompassing application of the term is problematic because it is at once too broad and too narrow. Such a sweeping definition allows skeptics to dismiss claims of racial profiling as "proof" of Black racial paranoia. A more appropriate label for this kitchen-sink approach is racial discrimination.

Government System Agents. A second application of racial profiling refers to the discriminatory use of race by government officials. This category includes the actions of any person who is linked to the government (federal or state). Racial targeting by any government agency, such as the Department of Justice, the Department of Health and Human Services, or state or municipal agencies, is included here. As well, this definition encompasses, but is not limited to, actions by police, judges, attorneys, and law enforcement officials. This category includes the selective use of race in traffic stops, border patrol checks, jury selection, closing arguments, and jury instructions.[4]

Police Officers in Traffic Stops. "Racial profiling" is often used to describe traffic stops by police officers. Even when the term is used to refer to a traffic stop, other questions remain. First, does it refer to the practice in which police use race as one factor in the decision to stop a motorist? Or, does it refer only to the practice in which police use race as the *sole* basis for making a motorist stop? While these questions pose an interesting point-counterpoint, it is unrealistic to suggest that race is commonly used as the sole basis for a motorist stop. The decision-making process is a nuanced one that involves considering many variables. Thus, the sole-factor debate is primarily theoretical, not practical. Notably, the single-factor approach supports the belief that profiling requires intentional racial bias, that is, only racists engage in racial profiling.[5]

On the issue of how race may be used in motorist stops, the U.S. Supreme Court has offered dimmers rather than fog lights. It has stated that police may use race as one of several factors in deciding whether to stop and question a suspect. As well, the Court has indicated that race cannot be used by an officer as the sole criterion for initiating a motorist stop.[6] On balance, however, the Court has apparently concluded that preserving police discretion is more important than determining the role race plays in an officer's calculus to initiate a traffic stop. The Court has bypassed several opportunities to squarely address the use of race by law enforcement officers.

Regardless of the approach, the issue of how to define race must be addressed, specifically, which groups are included within the discussion of profiling. The lion's share of the public talk, empirical analyses, and discussion of racial profiling has focused on African Americans. African Americans, however, are not the only racial group subjected to racial profiling. "DWB" has also been used as shorthand for "Driving while Brown"—a reference to Hispanics. There have been numerous reports of racially discriminatory treatment of Hispanic motorists by police. In one instance, four Birmingham, Alabama, police officers admitted to harassing and extorting money from Hispanic motorists. Between 1998 and 2000, the officers singled out Hispanics, whom they believed were more likely to carry cash and less likely to resist arrest because of possible immigration concerns.[7] There have been scores of other cases involving Hispanics and American Indians, who have also reported being subjected to race-based traffic stops.[8] As well, allegations of racial profiling have come from members of the Asian American community.[9]

The racial profiling of Arab and Middle Easterners (both American citizens and noncitizens) has increased greatly since the September 11, 2001, terrorist attacks on the World Trade Center and the Pentagon. In response to increased security fears, Americans have expressed strong support for the practice of race-based stops and searches. A September 2001 Gallup poll reported that 71 percent of Blacks expressed support for subjecting Arab Americans to "special" and "intensive" security checks at airports. This is an interesting finding considering that African Americans have consistently argued that racial profiling is a biased and unlawful practice. In the same Gallup survey, 57 percent of Whites expressed support for the enhanced scrutiny of Arab Americans.[10]

The above discussion highlights some of the meanings attributed to "racial profiling." The term refers to practices ranging from routine traffic stops in which race is the primary basis for the stop to surveillance of the movements of minority customers at retail stores. Such broad uses of "racial profiling" include actions taken by federal and state officers, as well as those by private individuals. Although there are varied definitions of racial profiling, the focus of this chapter is on racial bias in traffic stops by law enforcement officers. Both national events and research indicate that profiling by law enforcement deserves an analytical spotlight all its own.

III. Legislative and Legal Responses
to Racial Profiling of Motorists by Law Enforcement Officers

The Traffic Stops Statistics Study Act

The first piece of contemporary legislation proposed to address the problem of racial profiling was the 1997 Traffic Stops Statistics Study Act (TSSSA). The bill would have required that law enforcement officers collect data on each traffic stop. Specifically, it would have required information on the motorist's race, ethnicity, and age; the basis for the stop; whether a citation was issued; whether a search was conducted; the basis for the vehicle search and what, if anything, was discovered; and whether an arrest was made. Data would have been turned over to the U.S. attorney general, who would publish an annual summary. The TSSSA was approved by a unanimous vote in the House but did not pass the Senate. In 2000, John Conyers introduced a nearly identical version of the bill. Unlike the first version, it required information on the gender of the motorist, the number of people traveling in the vehicle, and whether the officer asked about the driver's immigration status. This legislation, too, was defeated.[11]

State and Local Action

The introduction of the TSSSA prompted several states to enact racial profiling legislation. More than twenty states have considered racial profiling legislation; the fourteen jurisdictions that mandate the collection of profiling data are Colorado, Connecticut, Kansas, Kentucky, Maryland, Massachusetts, Missouri, Nebraska, North Carolina, Oklahoma, Rhode Island, Tennessee, Texas, and Washington.[12] The Missouri statute is particularly noteworthy. This comprehensive law, passed in 2001, requires the collection of data for each motorist stop (e.g., race, gender age of motorist, reason for the stop). It goes further, however, to require the following:

- A determination of whether individual officers disproportionately stop minority motorists.
- Where a pattern is established, whether officers have used motorist stops as a pretext to investigate other criminal violations.[13]

- A requirement that officers who are found to have a pattern of targeting minority motorists receive appropriate counseling and training within ninety days. Counseling includes instruction that stresses respect for racial and cultural differences.
- Allocation of state funds to equip police vehicles with video cameras.[14]

Additionally, some police departments (e.g., Houston, San Diego, and San Jose) have initiated data collection procedures. Some jurisdictions have been partly driven by a desire to strengthen the relationship between police and minority communities.

For other police departments, the decision to collect statistics came from outside the department. In Montgomery County, Maryland, for example, data gathering began in response to complaints by the local NAACP. At the urging of the Justice Department, the St. Paul, Minnesota, Police Department and the NAACP reached an agreement; the police department agreed to monitor its early warning system to identify those officers who are likely to engage in racial profiling; enhance data collection on the incidence and prevalence of racial profiling; distribute business cards at all traffic stops; and provide a consent search advisory that requires the officer to inform the motorist that he has the right to refuse a request to search the vehicle.[15]

Legal Action

Lawsuits alleging unlawful profiling practices have also led to data collection on traffic stops. Cases have been filed on a variety of legislative and constitutional grounds, including the Due Process and Equal Protection clauses. Legal redress has been sought in various states, including Oklahoma, New Jersey, Maryland, Illinois, Florida, Pennsylvania, and Colorado.

Two cases, *Ledford v. City of Highland Park* and *Chavez v. Illinois State Police,* illustrate how racial profiling has been addressed in federal district courts.[16] *Ledford,* decided in 2000, involved a class-action lawsuit filed against Highland Park, a Chicago suburb. The American Civil Liberties Union brought the complaint on behalf of Michael Ledford; his mother, Karen Ledford; and the Black residents of Highland Park. The plaintiffs alleged that the Highland Park Police Department supported race-targeted traffic stops in violation of the Equal Protection Clause and

Title VI of the Civil Rights Act. They claimed that the police department maintained customs and practices that allowed or encouraged officers to target motorists on the basis of race or ethnicity.

In response to the lawsuit, the department entered into a consent decree. By its terms, officers are prohibited from using race "in any fashion or to any degree"[17] in their decision to stop or detain a suspect. Also, police are to gather statistical data on each traffic stop (including the motorist's race and gender; the basis for the stop; and the type of search). Also, for each stop, officers must record vehicle information. Last, each report must include the name and identification number of the police officer involved in the stop. In addition, the *Ledford* decree requires that police cars be equipped with audiovisual cameras; that officers inform each motorist stopped of his right to contest the stop; and that each officer report the profiling violations of other officers. These provisions appear to blueprint a responsive and tailored approach to profiling.

While *Ledford* suggests some forward steps, further changes are required. For example, additional information from police stops would be helpful, such as the race of the officer who made the stop and his age, gender, and length of time on the force. These data could be used to assess whether these factors affect the likelihood that an officer will engage in profiling. Also, an analysis of information on the make and type of vehicle would allow for a determination of whether newer or older model cars are more likely to be pulled over. The need for these data derives directly from claims by Black men that they are targeted on the basis of the vehicles they drive.

Chavez, a 2001 case, involved a claim that a special police unit of the Illinois Police Department was engaged in racial profiling. The plaintiffs alleged that the drug interdiction team, Operation Valkyrie, unlawfully singled out African American and Hispanic motorists in violation of the Equal Protection Clause and the Fourth Amendment's prohibition against unreasonable searches and seizures. Though the Seventh Circuit Court of Appeals found insufficient evidence to support a finding of racial profiling, it mapped out the empirical data that are required to prove such charges.

The court of appeals looked to the U.S. Supreme Court's 1996 decision in *U.S. v. Armstrong* for guidance.[18] In *Armstrong,* the Court addressed an alleged prosecutorial practice of prosecuting crack cocaine offenders (mostly African American) in federal court, rather than in state court, where the sanctions were less severe, while those arrested for powder cocaine–related offenses (mostly White) were being tried in state court. The *Armstrong* case held that some evidence of racial bias must be presented before the Court could require the U.S. attorney's office to disclose information that would reveal any racial bias in its prosecutions, including data on race of the defendants.

The *Chavez* court observed that, while *Armstrong* involved criminal charges, *Chavez* was a civil action—an important distinction given that the standard in a civil racial profiling case is lower than that for a criminal prosecution. In civil racial profiling cases, plaintiffs may use statistics to demonstrate that the police treated members of their race differently than other similarly situated motorists: "[S]tatistics demonstrating that whites stopped for traffic violations were not detained and searched . . . while similarly situated African American or Hispanic drivers were detained and searched, would be sufficient to show discriminatory intent."[19]

The Seventh Circuit noted that statistical data are useful in establishing the prevalence of profiling as well as providing the baseline for comparison. Determining the prevalence of racial profiling would ideally be founded upon data that are representative of motorists who drive and those who have been stopped. To properly interpret these figures, the plaintiff must use an accurate population benchmark. The standard population reference—the percentage of the general population that is made up of members of a particular racial group—is misleading. The court observed that census figures for racial minorities are widely known to be undercounts and therefore are unreliable. It concluded that a successful racial profiling claim requires that the plaintiff provide reliable data on the number of motorists traveling on Illinois interstate highways.

Together, *Ledford* and *Chavez* demonstrate the benefits and limits of legal action. *Ledford* signals the willingness of at least one circuit court to hear and respond to racial profiling charges, while *Chavez* outlines a high minimum threshold for a successful legal challenge.

End Racial Profiling Act of 2001[20]

The End Racial Profiling Act of 2001 (ERPA) was introduced to sanction racial profiling. Notably, it differs in scope, focus, and tone from the TSSSA. First, the ERPA would prohibit law enforcement agents and agencies from engaging in racial profiling. Second, the legislation would permit the United States, or an individual who has been harmed by racial profiling, to sue for declaratory or injunctive relief in state or federal court. Notably, however, it would not allow a victim of racial profiling to collect money damages. Third, the proposed law states that racial profiling violates the Equal Protection Clause, the Interstate Commerce Clause, and the Fourth Amendment. Relying upon motions to suppress illegally obtained evidence to deter racial profiling is ineffective; for example, where there has been an unlawful search and seizure and no contraband is found, there will be no arrest, no case, and, therefore, no motion to suppress. Even with its limitations, however, the ERPA may provide some measure of redress for racial profiling. Hearings on the bill were held in August 2001; however, the legislation was not passed.

IV. Empirical Analyses of Racial Profiling

The action taken by the states and by the federal government has not been accompanied by a comparable amount of research interest. Very few empirical studies have focused on profiling. As the discussion below indicates, although there is clear evidence that profiling exists, more detailed empirical analyses should be done.

Maryland Study. In the late 1990s, John Lamberth and his colleagues compared the racial distribution of motorists traveling on an interstate highway with the race of motorists stopped on the highway by state troopers.[21] The study, based on searches conducted between January 1995 and September 1997, is divided into two parts. The first part reviews the law enforcement records for the Maryland State Police. These data cover stops conducted between May and September 1997. During this period, police made 11,823 vehicle stops. Sixty-four percent involved White drivers, 29 percent African Americans, and 2 percent Hispanics. Lamberth also examined statistics on those vehicles that were subject to a police search. Here, the racial pattern was reversed: 71 percent of the motorists whose vehicles were searched were African American, while 21 percent were White and 2 percent were Hispanic.

The second part of the study was designed to determine the racial characteristics of motorists on Interstate 95. Statistics were gathered, by observation, on the race of motorists who were traveling on the highway and on the race of motorists who were traveling over the speed limit. Researchers were able to identify motorists in 97 percent of the cases. Lamberth and his colleagues found that 76 percent of the drivers were White and 17 percent were African American. Of those motorists who were observed violating traffic laws (e.g., speeding), 75 percent were White and 18 percent were African American. On the basis of these findings, Lamberth concluded that African American motorists violate interstate traffic laws at a rate proportional to their presence in the interstate driving population. However, they found, African Americans were stopped at almost two times their rate of travel and are more than four times as likely to have their vehicles searched.

Florida Study. In this study, David Harris analyzed videotaped motorist stops (gathered over a three-year period) along a section of the Interstate 95 corridor in Volusia County, Florida. The videotaped data indicate that officers conducted more than 1,100 vehicle stops. The stops were for traffic violations, such as speeding, swerving, failing to use signals, or displaying improper tags. Seventy percent of the motorists subjected to stops were African American or Hispanic. Approximately 50 percent of the cars that were pulled over were searched, and 80 percent of the cars searched were driven by someone African American or Hispanic. Harris also found that the duration of the stops for minority motorists was twice as long as that for White motorists. Notably, fewer than 10 of the 1,100 motorists who were stopped received tickets. Harris compared these data with population statistics. He found that African Americans comprised less than 12 percent of the driving age population and approximately 15 percent of the driving traffic offenders in the state. Overall, Harris concluded that Black motorists are subject to vehicle stops at a disproportionately higher rate.

Philadelphia ACLU Monitoring Report. This report analyzes the racial characteristics of motorists who were stopped in several Philadelphia police districts in 1997. In some instances, data for vehicle and pedestrian stops are combined. The results indicate that where information on motorist's race was available, minorities were disproportionately overrepresented. Specifically, minorities were more likely to be subject to stops that were later judged by a court to be baseless.[22]

New Jersey Attorney General's Report. This 1999 study reviews data collected by the New Jersey State Police. It includes information gathered in the course of more than eighty-seven thousand motorist stops, searches, and arrests made during the mid- to late 1990s along the New Jersey Turnpike. The study reports that 59 percent of the drivers who were stopped were White, 27 percent were Black, and 7 percent were Hispanic. Of the 1,193 motorists who consented to a vehicle search, 53 percent were African American, 21 percent White, and 24 percent Hispanic. Further, of the three thousand vehicle stops that resulted in an arrest, 62 percent involved Black motorists and 32 percent involved White.[23]

The report concluded that the New Jersey State Police used race as a factor in determining whether to make a vehicle stop. It was determined that a small group of officers was engaging in willful misconduct.[24] Police officers as a group were influenced by negative stereotypes of minorities, which in turn affected law enforcement practices.

Prevalence of Profiling. A published study by Richard Lundman and Robert Kaufman uses data from the 1999 National Crime Victimization Survey to examine the prevalence of racial profiling. The researchers focused on the 7,034 survey participants who had been stopped by the police one or more times in the previous year. Specifically, they explored the prevalence of traffic stops and the motorists' perceptions of these stops. Lundman and Kaufman found that although there was no significant difference in find rates (discovery of contraband) between Black and White men, Black men were 33 percent more likely to be stopped by police than White men. In fact, Whites were more likely to be found with contraband (13.8 percent) than Blacks (11.4 percent). They also found that one-third of those Blacks surveyed believed they had been unfairly pulled over, compared with one-fifth of Whites and one-fourth of Latinos.[25]

These five studies are among the first empirical analyses of racial profiling. They indicate that Black motorists are more likely to be stopped than motorists from other racial groups. The studies conclude that the high stop rate for Black motorists is not explained by legally relevant variables. It is noted that Hispanics, too, are disproportionately overrepresented in traffic stops. Because there are key differences in the research designs and analyses used in these studies, more empirical research is necessary, including follow-up studies of those police departments that have gathered profiling data and have implemented strategic procedural responses. Given that most traffic stops are carried out by local police, it is important to examine their actions with respect to racial profiling. As well, it is important to broaden the research focus to include Hispanics, Asian Americans, and American Indians.

V. *DWB and Its Kin*

Racial profiling offers a point of entry for analyzing how Blackness is equated with deviance. This section outlines some of the ways that having Black skin exacts a social cost. There is a surreal list of ways that Blackness has evoked criminal suspicion. The volume and range of these "living while Black" encounters makes it impossible to dismiss them as racial paranoia.[26]

Walking while Black. In a May 2000 essay published in the *Village Voice*, Bryonn Bain, a twenty-two-year-old African American who had recently completed his first year at Harvard Law School, describes an incident in which he and two relatives, after having observed a crime, were mistaken for the criminal suspects.[27] The action taken by the New York police led Bain to conclude that there is a "special Bill of Rights for nonwhite people in the United States, one that applies with particular severity to Black men."[28] Using incendiary prose, Bain offers his real-world version of the Bill of Rights for Blacks: Blacks are explicitly denied full citizenship; Blacks do not have the right to travel outside of their neighborhoods; Blacks may be arrested on less than probable cause; Whites may arrest Blacks for suspected criminal activity; and Blacks are not entitled to due process. Bain persuasively argues that this is the contemporary reality for many African Americans, particularly young men.

Others have chronicled comparable experiences. For example, Paul Butler, an African American law professor in Washington, D.C., describes his experience of being stopped, questioned, and harassed by police for "walking while Black." One evening as he returned home to his predominantly White, middle-class neighborhood in northwest D.C., he was stopped by police, who insisted that he provide them with identification. Butler, who was on foot, refused. The standoff ended only after a neighbor vouched for Butler.[29]

Standing while Black. Chicago v. Morales[30] offers an example of how standing while Black has been criminalized. This 1999 case involved a statute that made it a crime for gang members, or anyone associated with them, to stand on a public street. According to the law, police could stop anyone "reasonably believe[d] to be a criminal street gang member loitering in any public place with one or more other persons."[31] While the ordinance was in effect, Chicago police arrested more than forty-two thousand people for violating the ordinance. The U.S. Supreme Court held that the statute was unconstitutional (see chapter 1 for a more detailed discussion of this case).

Standing in an Apartment Vestibule while Black. In February 1999, Amadou Diallo, a Guinean immigrant, was shot and killed by four New York City police officers. Police fired forty-one shots at Mr. Diallo, who was unarmed, as he stood in the vestibule of his apartment building. Police wrongly suspected Diallo of rape. Undercover officers fired at Diallo after he reached toward his pants pocket; the police mistook the wallet he held up for them to see for a handgun. A year following the shooting death, the four officers charged in the case were acquitted of any criminal wrongdoing.

Hailing a Cab while Black. Long touted as an acute problem for African American men living in urban areas, the reluctance of taxi cab drivers to accept Black fares was given new legs when the actor Danny Glover said that he and his daughter were continually passed up for cab service in New York.[32]

Shopping while Black. A case involving three Black teenagers is among the more remarkable incidents of "shopping while Black." On October 20, 1995, the high schoolers visited a new Eddie Bauer outlet in suburban Maryland. The store security guard (an off-duty policeman) suspected that one of them, Alonzo Jackson, had stolen the shirt he was wearing. When questioned by store employees, the sixteen-year-old Jackson stated that he had purchased the shirt the previous day. The store clerks did not believe Jackson's story. He was told that he would have to remove the shirt he was wearing before he would be permitted to exit the store. Jackson took off his shirt and left the premises wearing his undershirt. He returned later that evening with the purchase receipt and retrieved his shirt. Following the incident, the three youths filed a civil rights law suit against Eddie Bauer. They were awarded $1 million in damages.[33]

Running while Black. The case of *Illinois v. Wardlow*[34] involved the police search and seizure of a young Black man. At the sight of police, Wardlow, who was standing in a high-drug-traffic area, fled quickly on foot. The officers observed that Wardlow held an opaque bag in his hand and gave chase. Police caught Wardlow, and, during the patdown, they discovered a gun and ammunition. Wardlow's attorney argued that the search was not based upon reasonable suspicion and, therefore, violated the Fourth Amendment. The U.S. Supreme Court held that, although flight cannot be equated with guilt, unprovoked flight, combined with presence in a neighborhood known for its drug traffic, is sufficient to justify a police patdown under the Fourth Amendment.

Idling while Black. In December 1998, Tyisha Miller, a nineteen-year-old Black woman, was shot and killed by Riverside, California, police, after they responded to a call. Miller was seated in her parked car at a gas station after discovering a problem with one of her tires. When police arrived, they discovered that the car doors were locked, the engine was running, and Miller, who appeared to be unconscious, had a gun in her lap. The police responded by breaking Miller's car window and firing into the vehicle. Miller, who was struck twelve times in the head and back, died.[35]

Breathing while Black.[36] This phrase has been used to describe the outcome of an Oneonta, New York, case. In September 1992, someone broke into the home of a seventy-seven-year-old White woman and assaulted her with a knife. The victim did not see her attacker's face. She told police that, on the basis of her observation of the assailant's arm, she believed he was an African American male. She also stated that, on the basis of how quickly the assailant walked across the room, she believed that he was young. The victim also told police that in the struggle, the attacker unintentionally cut his hand with the knife. Police used a canine to track the attacker's scent. The trail led them toward the State University College of New York (SUCO), where 2 percent of the students were African American. Police then requested a list of the school's Black male students. A list was supplied, and the police questioned more than two hundred Black men from the college and the adjoining town. During the questioning, the men's hands were inspected for cuts. The constitutional challenges to these actions were dismissed by the Second Circuit. In 2001, the U.S. Supreme Court declined to hear the case.[37]

These examples demonstrate how the link between Blackness and deviance intersects with policing. Notably, the above list is not exhaustive. Among the more notorious examples of living while Black is the 1999 race-based roundup of African Americans in Tulia, Texas.[38] Based upon the uncorroborated testimony of a single undercover agent, Tulia, Texas, police arrested more than forty Blacks—approximately 16 percent of

Tulia's Black population—in an undercover drug sting. The majority of these cases led to convictions and sentences. An investigation by the state special prosecutor revealed that the evidence was unreliable and all convictions were voided. Later, thirty-one Blacks were pardoned. All told, racial profiling is best viewed as a social problem, not simply as a policing problem. Equally important, racial profiling has a host of corollary harms and collateral consequences. Some of these are considered in the next section.

VI. *"Truth" and Racial Consequences*

As the incidents of living while Black described in the preceding section attest, sometimes Black skin is equated with deviance. Far from operating in a vacuum, this problem has tangible costs and consequences. Some of these costs—legal, social, and political—are discussed in this section.

Linking Abortion and Crime

During the spring of 1999, an unpublished paper by John Donohue and Steven Levitt began making the rounds within academic circles. The paper, "Legalized Abortion and Crime," analyzes the impact of the U.S. Supreme Court's 1973 decision in *Roe v. Wade,* which legalized abortion.[39] Specifically, Donohue and Levitt consider whether there is a relationship between the increased rate of abortions in the early 1990s (the generation that has come of age since *Roe* was decided) and the sharp decrease in the crime rate between 1991 and 1997. They conclude that a causal link exists: "Legalized abortion can account for about half the observed decline in crime in the United States between 1991 and 1997."[40] For support, Donohue and Levitt refer to research that establishes a link between family environment and future criminality. They attribute the remaining half of the drop to sentencing and incarceration policies.

Donohue and Levitt observe that abortion is most common for poor, young, minority women. Quoting one study, they note that "[W]hile abortion reforms had relatively modest effects on the fertility of white women, 'black women who were exposed to abortion reforms experienced large reductions in teen fertility and teen out-of-wedlock fertility.'"[41] Further, the increased availability of abortion decreased the number of low-birth weight, at-risk babies.

Considering the study's potential policy implications, it received relatively little press attention. Most of the news reports provided a summary of the findings but few went beyond a restatement of its conclusions. Academia, however, has critiqued Donohue and Levitt's research.[42]

It is difficult to select the appropriate place to begin an analysis of Donohue and Levitt's article. Several issues are raised by the research itself, as well as its potential consequences for social policy. First, does the study represent eugenics disguised as scholarship? The fairly direct bottom line of Donohue and Levitt's findings is that the availability of abortion in the early 1970s (combined with tougher sentencing guidelines) dramatically reduced the U.S. crime rate. The authors note in passing that their research is neither an endorsement of abortion nor a call for state intervention into the reproductive decisions of women. In response to concerns about policy implications, Donohue has commented, "I don't think it's our job as economists or scientists to withhold truth because some people are not going to like it. I just think it's important to understand the impact of social policies."[43] Given the researchers' conclusion that legalized abortion account for approximately one-half of the crime drop, some discussion of what policy might flow from these findings is a reasonable expectation. Their failure to directly address these issues does not void the question of whether their research supports race-based eugenics.

Second, there is the issue of "statistical discrimination."[44] Donohue and Levitt's line of reasoning encourages the use of a broad criminal brush to paint the children of poor, Black teenagers. Notably, most of the children born to poor, unmarried Black women are not involved in crime. Thus, one potential consequence of the study is the assignment of group blame—holding the cohort of young, minority, poor mothers responsible for the nation's crime problem.

Third, an analysis of how the abortion rate factors into the crime rate is a back-end approach. Donohue and Levitt's research suggests that encouraging poor, minority women to have abortions may be a successful crime prevention strategy. However, they also correctly observe that conditions such as poverty, low level of education, and single parenthood are highly correlated with future criminality. An ideal strategy for reducing the crime rate would start with addressing these root causes first, before discussing abortion practices. Focusing on the underlying conditions that nurture criminality is a more direct and proactive strategy for addressing the crime problem.

Fourth, taking the study's findings at face value, they tell only part of the story. Donohue and Levitt focus exclusively on street crime (e.g., violent and property offenses). One question that arises is whether there is a relationship between levels of white-collar and corporate offending and the legalization of abortion. It is this query that shines light on the heart of Donohue and Levitt's work: Would we consider posing the same research question for white-collar and corporate criminals, who are overwhelmingly White men?

Whether intended or unintended, the conclusion logically deduced from Donohue and Levitt's research is that women who are poor, unmarried, and African American should be encouraged to abort. In fact, on the basis of these research findings, these women appear to have a duty to abort. After all, they are the group of mothers most likely to raise criminals. Thus, Donohue and Levitt's study offers yet another twist on the Blackness-as-deviance phenomenon detailed earlier—"viable while Black."

The "CRACK" Antidote: Linking Birth Control and Crime

Social and political interest in Black female reproduction is not new. During American slavery, Black female pregnancy was encouraged and celebrated by Whites as an economically beneficial event. Over decades, however, the disproportionately high birth rate of Blacks has received closer scrutiny and has been widely viewed as a form of social deviance. More recently, the disproportionately high reproductive rates for African American women has caused alarm, as evidenced by a wide array of legislative policies. Donohue and Levitt's research represents one kind of evaluation of and response to Black birth rates. Their research, a step removed from policy implementation, makes an empirical case for scrutinizing pregnancy outcomes for Black women. Others, such as the practices involved in the CRACK program and the practices challenged in the *Ferguson v. Charleston* case,[45] encourage a more direct response to the high Black birth rate.

Barbara Harris is the founder of Children Requiring a Caring Kommunity (CRACK). Her organization offers drug-addicted women two hundred dollars in cash in exchange for a tubal ligation or long-term contraception, such as Norplant or Depo-Provera. Harris, who is White, is the adoptive mother of four Black children. Harris arrived at the idea for the CRACK program after learning about a drug-addicted Black woman who gave birth to several children.[46] Harris's plan was to make it unlawful for poor, drug-addicted women to bear children. CRACK has offices in Anaheim and in Chicago. Program billboards have been posted in several states, including Minnesota, Pennsylvania, Florida, New Hampshire, and Michigan. By June 2000, 237 people had participated in the program, 236 women and one man. Approximately one-half were Black, and one-half were White; there were 102 Black participants, 101 Whites, six people classified as biracial, and three as Indian.[47] Fifty percent of the women in the program agreed to the tubal procedure. The CRACK program is funded primarily by private donations.

The scrutiny of poor, drug-dependent pregnant women has gone beyond attempts to sterilization them. Numerous states have taken steps to impose criminal sanctions. The state action challenged in *Ferguson* provides an interesting example of one state's attempts to identify and arrest poor, cocaine-addicted pregnant women. At issue was a practice by the Medical University of South Carolina (MUSC) in conjunction with the Charleston solicitor, Charles Condon. Condon, after being contacted by the MUSC attorney, developed a policy that permitted drug testing for pregnant women. The policy identified who would be tested, what steps would be taken once a urine sample was obtained, and what information (education and referral) was to be given to women who tested positive. Per the policy, the police were to be notified and an arrest made if there was a second positive drug test or if the woman missed a meeting with a substance abuse counselor. Women who tested positive and were more than twenty-seven weeks pregnant were charged with drug possession and distribution to a minor; they had to either consent to treatment for substance abuse or face arrest.

Ten women who had been arrested and prosecuted under the Charleston policy argued that they had been subject to an unconstitutional search in violation of the Fourth Amendment. The U.S. Supreme Court agreed. The *Ferguson* Court weighed the privacy interests of the pregnant woman against the states' interest in crime control. The Court held that the Charleston practice, which was designed to "generate evidence for enforcement purposes," was a clear violation of the women's privacy rights and did not fall within the "special needs" exception to the Fourth Amendment.

Corollary Consequences: Legal, Policy, and Social Issues

In addition to its apparently direct impact on research and social programs, the "living while Black" phenomenon has corollary consequences. Two incidents are used to illustrate this point. *United States v. Leviner* provides the first example.[48] In this case, federal district judge Nancy Gertner issued a downward departure in the federal sentencing guidelines. It is the judge's reasoning for the reduction that makes this otherwise unremarkable case remarkable. Alexander Leviner was a passenger in a car that was pulled over for speeding and because it lacked headlights. The police had received a report of shots fired in the area. After discovering a discrepancy in the vehicle registration, the officers had the driver and passengers step outside the car. Leviner was searched, and police discovered a gun holster in the vehicle. A gun was later found outside the vehicle. Leviner, who had several prior convictions, was charged under the federal sentencing guidelines as being a felon in possession of a firearm. On the basis of his criminal history, Leviner was a "Category V" offender, the second highest ranking.

After reviewing the record, Judge Gertner made two observations. First, Leviner was Black. Second, most of his prior convictions were for motor vehicle offenses initiated by traffic stops. Gertner stated:

> Motor vehicle offenses, in particular, raise deep concerns about racial disparity. Studies from a number of scholars and articles in the popular literature have focused on the fact that African-American motorists are stopped and prosecuted for traffic stops, more than any other citizens. And if that is so, then it is not unreasonable to believe that African Americans would also be imprisoned at a higher rate for those offenses as well.[49]

The opinion outlines how a strict application of the federal guidelines would work a rough justice in Leviner's case. In reaching a sentencing decision, Judge Gertner considered several factors, including the defendant's stable employment history and close family bonds and the fact that one of his convictions (which the prosecution used to support an enhanced sentence) was issued *after* his arrest for the shooting charge. Based on this, Judge Gertner rejected the federal guidelines and sentenced Leviner to thirty months in prison.

It is not known whether other judges have taken action similar to that of Judge Gertner. It is known, however, that in other contexts, federal judges have sought relief from harsh sentences with racially disparate outcomes, particularly those related to the possession and distribution of cocaine. More than a few federal judges have balked at the disparity between crack and powder cocaine sentences and noted the racial impact this disparity creates. Some judges have resigned in protest, while others have apologized to defendants in advance of sentencing.[50]

A case involving the National Urban League provides the second example of how the failure to address the risks of "living while Black" affects social policy. In 1998, the Urban League withdrew from the Clinton administration's "Buckle Up America" campaign. The effort, which would have made the failure to wear a safety belt a primary traffic offense, would permit police officers to stop and ticket motorists for neglecting to wear their seat belts. The Urban League declined to support the campaign after concluding that it might increase the number of African Americans who would be subjected to racial profiling.

The Urban League's response is problematic, given that young Black and Hispanic motorists are twice as likely as their White counterparts to die in automobile crashes because they fail to wear seat belts. Further, the failure to address the problem of seat belt use in minority communities increases the probability of not only higher mortality rates but also increased auto insurance premiums and hospital costs for crash-related injuries. The Urban League's response demonstrates that the problem of living while Black extends beyond the criminal justice system and impacts support for social policies. This stance has the potential to create as much harm as it seeks to prevent.

In addition to political and legal costs, there are personal costs associated with profiling. Those who have been subjected to profiling tell stories of fear, alienation, and self-doubt. Not surprisingly, this affects their behavior. David Harris comments, "It may cause people of color to plan their driving and travel routes in certain ways, to take . . . particular jobs, even to wear clothing and behave in ways that minimize their potential to attract police attention."[51]

VII. In Conclusion: The Big Picture

Based on the above discussion, three observations are made. First, there are overlapping and conflicting meanings attached to the term "racial profiling." As a consequence, those who address profiling should provide a clear definition of the term. Specifically, whether it is a reference to police practices that include race as indicative of criminal suspicion, a general reference to being singled out in a public space (e.g., at a store or airport) on the basis of race, or a generic reference to the problem of assigning deviance to an entire racial group. Given the various instances in which Black skin has been mistaken for criminality—including the nonexhaustive list of living while Black examples—it is understandable that the term "racial profiling" has numerous contextual meanings. A fruitful dialogue, however, requires that care be taken to differentiate between those uses. The failure to do so is not only confusing; it also allows racial profiling to be dismissed as rhetoric, rather than viewed as a social problem.

Second, the use of race as a proxy for deviance is not limited to racial profiling by law enforcement officers. Other examples include the argument that legalized abortion is somehow linked to crime and race and the CRACK program. Beyond these, however, there are indirect and unintended outcomes of the failure to address both racial profiling by police officers and the ready association between dark skin and deviance. A story told at a 1998 criminal justice conference illustrates the problem of unintended consequences. During a panel session on policing, a White professor said that he had been contacted by the owner of a country club. The owner needed help with a problem: All of his Black workers were quitting. The employees had complained of being frequently stopped and harassed by the local police as they traveled to work. Apparently, officers became suspicious whenever Blacks were seen driving or walking in the exclusive section of town. The club owner's goal in contacting the professor was to determine whether there was some way to label his Black employees as "good" Blacks—ones who should not be subjected to profiling. The impact of profiling on a business spotlights yet another unintended outcome of racial profiling practices.

Third, existing measures for addressing racial profiling are reactive. Judge Gertner's response in the *Leviner* case offers a powerful example. As noted, it is likely that there have been other legal decision makers who have considered the prevalence of racial profiling in their individual case assessments and decisions. As well, other legal actors, such as judges—either because they are not familiar with the empirical literature on profiling or because they dispute its relevance—may not factor in the possibility of racial profiling when deciding on an appropriate sentence. Not surprisingly, these varied responses create the potential for even greater variability in the sentencing process.

In sum, profiling schemes, ostensibly designed to solve one set of problems (e.g., crime), create a host of others. Placing people into groups on the basis of skin tone has a number of harmful and unanticipated outcomes. These include fostering interracial hostility, further damaging police-minority community relations, and increasing the inequities that face various racial minorities in the criminal justice system.

7

Black Women
and the Justice System
Raced and Gendered into Submission

I. Introduction

Without fail, most of the studies on Black women and the criminal justice system begin by noting that there is little research on the topic. The small body of research that does exist has not attracted much attention. Why is this? One possibility: Black women occupy a unique space in the public and academic consciousness. In contrast to that for Black males, the locus for public discussion of Black female deviance is not in reports of crime. For Black women, it is deviance of another kind that carries the day. They are alternately represented as leeches (welfare recipients), pilferers (welfare queens), or undeserving employees (affirmative-action beneficiaries), or, more generally, as irresponsible, promiscuous young women who are ready, willing, and able to become out-of-wedlock mothers.[1] These compelling stereotypical portrayals have obscured the equally compelling reality of Black women and the justice system: Black women are the fastest-growing race and gender group within the justice system.

While Black men are the poster children for the justice system, Black women remain off-center, blurry background figures. The underground, coded message is subtle, yet clear. Black women do not merit widespread criminological attention. This reflects a discipline-wide emphasis on disproportionately high offense rates for men in general and Black men in particular. As one researcher observes, "[C]riminology is in possession of one of the most consistently demonstrated findings in all of the social sciences. As long as statistics have been collected, they have revealed that men are considerably more likely than women to engage in [crime]."[2] Over the past few decades, there has been a concerted effort, particularly by feminist scholars, to bring women into the empirical and theoretical fold. An outgrowth of this has been the development of new theories and perspectives explaining women's involvement in the justice system. In an incisive essay on what she terms "intersectionality," Kimberlé Crenshaw argues for rejecting rigid, formulaic categories, such as those of race and gender, to explain crime and victimization.[3] This outside-the-box thinking, Crenshaw argues, is required to "see" the category of "Black female" as separate and distinct from "Black male" or "White female."

The first section of this chapter presents an overview and critique of the existing research on Black women and the justice system. The second part reviews historical and contemporary statistics on Black women's arrest and incarceration. The third section examines Black women's offense patterns. The fourth part provides a look at criminal victimization rates for Black women. The fifth section evaluates the existing theory on Black female offending. The sixth part discusses the research void on Black women and how the gap could be addressed. The chapter concludes with recommendations for bringing Black women's involvement in crime—theory and research—to the fore. Throughout the discussion, tables are used to illustrate the breadth and depth of Black women's involvement in the criminal justice system.

II. The Research Black Hole

Someone attempting to gather data on Black women and crime will quickly realize that she is in a research free fall. There is no established starting point—e.g., seminal document or book—for statistics on Black women and crime. To effectively review the literature, one must consult dozens of resources, including government reports, city- and state-level analyses, victimization surveys, journal articles, books, book chapters, and dissertations.[4] A review of these sources is the minimum required to piece together the most basic sketch of Black women and criminality. This multipronged research strategy is necessary because there are neither annual nor interim government reports on the state of Black women in the justice system. Notably, however, the Justice Department has published reports on young Black men and the justice system, and on women and crime.[5]

Missing Data and Other Concerns. Another research roadblock is that some of the standard resources for crime data do not provide specific information on Black women. For example, the Uniform Crime Reports, the bible on crime in the United States, does not include race-by-gender breakdowns in its annual arrest statistics. There are national data available on Black arrest rates, which are reported separately from national data on arrest rates for women. Data on Black women as a group, however, are not available. Related to this, there are information gaps within the existing sources. For example, a search for early-twentieth-century incarceration figures reveals that statistics are available for some years and not others. These empirical gaps make for incomplete historical analyses of Black women's experiences within the criminal justice system. Although the problem of missing data is not unique to research on Black women, it makes rocky an already encumbered path.

Further, there is the problem of matching data. It is difficult to track how Black women fare in criminal justice system processing—that is, from arrest to incarceration. For instance, locating arrest, offense, conviction, and sentence statistics for Black women in a particular jurisdiction and for a particular time period is a challenge. While these data are not readily available for any groups, for Black women, more digging is required. Again, the point is that obtaining data is harder than one would expect for the race and gender group with the criminal justice system's fastest-growing population.[6] One must travel a maze-like path to create a rudimentary statistical portrait of Black women and crime. Once the pieces are assembled, however, the picture that emerges is a stark one.

Research Tracks. Research on Black women and the justice system can be divided into two broad tracks or categories. The first category includes research that falls under the heading of "race and crime." In this category, the research is primarily focused on Black men. Although this strain of research purports to be about crime and race, it focuses primarily on Black male offending and victimization, it treats race and crime as synonymous with Black men.

The second track includes data classified under gender and crime. For the most part this research focuses on White women; it equates gender and crime with White women. The studies in this category are more accurately characterized as research on White women and the justice system. Within this category, Black women are largely treated as research footnotes.

The second group also includes studies that focus exclusively on Black women and crime. This research tends to involve small samples and to utilize qualitative research designs (e.g., in-depth interviews, focus groups). Though this constitutes a relatively small body of work, it is diverse. For the most part, these studies are not analyses of national-level data. Rather, they are a collection of state-, city-, program-, or population-specific studies. The next section reviews the existing research on Black women and the criminal justice system. It begins with a historical look at Black women's incarceration.

III. In the System

Some Historical Notes. The incarceration rate for Black women was high during the early twentieth century. Though data are not available for each year, existing figures paint a vivid portrait of female incarceration during the first part of the last century. Table 7-1 and table 7-2 highlight the criminal involvement of Black and White women in 1910 and between 1926 and 1946. In 1910, the incarceration rate for Black women was six times higher than the rate for White women. The incarceration rate for Black women was 418.3 per 100,000, while the rate for White women was 70 per 100,000. Notably, Black women made up almost one-half of the incarcerated female population (43 percent).

The high incarceration rates for Black females (adults and juveniles) continued throughout the first half of the 1900s. Between 1926 and 1946, Black women accounted for 31 percent of the incarcerated female population. By the end of the period, however, the rate reached a high of 40 percent, in 1946. Notably, as the rate increased for Black women, the rate for White women declined. During this twenty-one year period, White women constituted the largest percentage of the incarcerated female population in 1927 (75.2 percent); they made up the smallest percentage in 1946 (59 percent). On average, White women made up 63.3 percent of the incarcerated female population. These statistics, discussed in the following section, serve as a harbinger for Black women's contemporary rates of involvement in the justice system.

Contemporary Control Rates. "Control rate" refers to the percentage of a population that is under the jurisdiction of the criminal justice system— on probation, parole, in jail, or in prison. It provides a snapshot of a

TABLE 7-1

Female Prisoners and Juvenile Delinquents by Race, 1910

	Prisoners and Juveniles	Rate Per 100,000
Black Women	20,670	418.3
White Women	27,685	70

Source: U.S. Census (1969), Negro Population, 1790–1915, table 1, p. 436; table 19, p. 445.

TABLE 7-2

Female Prisoners by Race Entering State and Federal Prisons, 1926–1946.

	Total Female Prison Population	Black Females		White Females	
		#	%	#	%
1926	2,727	798	29.3%	1,827	67%
1927[a]	2,835	751	21.1%	2,048	75.2%
1928	2,780	741	27%	1,994	72%
1929	3,322	914	27%	2,364	71%
1930	3,056	863	28%	2,153	70%
1931	3,037	836	27%	2,165	71%
1932	2,931	791	27%	2,084	71%
1933	2,728	784	29%	1,910	70%
1934	2,974	840	28%	2,090	70%
1935	3,154	962	30%	2,161	68%
1936[b]	2,970	925	31%	2,016	68%
1937	3,218	1,056	33%	2,130	66%
1938	3,259	1,080	33%	2,155	66%
1939	3,395	1,189	35%	2,175	64%
1940	3,713	1,435	39%	2,237	60%
1941	3,190	1,172	37%	1,974	62%
1942	3,468	1,259	36%	2,158	62%
1943[c]	2,048	803	39%	1,225	60%
1944	2,176	811	37%	1,339	61%
1945	2,429	779	32%	1,628	67%
1946	2,889	1,150	40%	1,714	59%

Source: Department of Commerce, Bureau of the Census (1929), "Prisoners in State and Federal Prisons and Reformatories" (1926–1946, 4 bound volumes).

[a] The Census Bureau notes that these figures undercount Black prisoners. In 1927, eleven states did not submit data on prison admissions. Nine of these were southern states, which had high Black prison populations.
[b] Data on sentence completion indicate variation by race. Blacks were more likely to be incarcerated for the entire length of their sentence, whereas Whites were more likely to receive an early release (Bureau of the Census, 1936, p. 72).
[c] The Census Bureau notes that figures for 1943–1946 are incomplete. Specifically, there were no data submitted for Georgia between 1943 and 1946 and none for Michigan and Mississippi between 1942 and 1945.

group's overall involvement in the justice system. Black women make up 7 percent of the U.S. population and 13.5 percent of the female population.[7] For each criminal justice system indicator, the percentage of Black women under the supervision of the justice system far exceeds their percentage in the female population. On average, the control rate for Black women is six times greater than the control rate for White women.

Most striking, the rate for Black women is the highest and fastest-growing of all race and gender groups. Between 1989 and 1994, their rate rose more swiftly than the rate for Black men, White men, and Hispanic men (table 7-3). During this five-year period, the control rate for Black women jumped by 78 percent, making their increase 2.5 times greater than the increase for Black men, which was 31 percent. During the same period, the increase in control rates for other groups were as follows: White males, 8 percent; White females, 40 percent; Hispanic males and females, 18 percent each.[8]

Table 7-4 offers a more detailed look at women's control rates by race. The table provides a composite sketch of prison, jail, and probation rates. Overall, Black women constitute the largest group of incarcerated women

TABLE 7-3

Women and Men in the Criminal Justice System,
Percentages by Race, 1989 and 1994

		1989	1994	Percent Increase
Men	White	6.2%	6.7%	8%
	Black	23%	30.2%	31%
	Hispanic	10.4%	12.3%	18%
Women	White	1%	1.4%	40%
	Black	2.7%	4.8%	78%
	Hispanic	1.8%	2.2%	18%

Source: Mauer & Huling (1995), "Young African Americans and the Criminal Justice System."

TABLE 7-4

Adult Women in Prison, Jail, or on Probation, Percentages, 1998

	Probation	Jail	State Prison	Federal Prison
White	62%	36%	33%	29%
Black	27%	44%	48%	35%
Hispanic	10%	15%	15%	32%
Other	1%	5%	4%	4%

Source: Bureau of Justice Statistics, "Women Offenders," (October 2000), p. 7.

TABLE 7-5

Sentenced Women in State and Federal Prisons, by Race, 2001

	Number	Rate per 100,000
White Women	36,200	36
Black Women	36,400	199
Hispanic Women	10,200	61
Total	82,800	

Source: U.S. Department of Justice (2002), "Prisoners 2001," p. 12, tables 15, 16.

in state prison, federal prison, and jail, by race, for 1989 and 1994. As indicated, approximately 50 percent of the women serving time in state prison and 44 percent of those in jail are Black.[9] One-third of the women serving time in federal prison are Black. The lowest control rate for African American women is probation—27 percent. By contrast, the highest control rate for White women is probation—62 percent. This racial disparity is notable given that probation is both the least severe sanction within the justice system and the one most frequently meted out.

Table 7-5 provides the statistics on the number of women sentenced to state and federal prison in 2001. Of the 82,800 women who were sentenced, 36,200, or 44 percent, were Black. White women also make up 44 percent of this group; Hispanic females account for 12 percent (10,200).[10] A look at sentencing rates by race indicates clear disparities. Per 100,000 people, the sentencing rate for Black women is 199, 61 for Hispanic women, and 36 for White women. Thus, the rate for Black women is more than five times the rate for White women and more than three times the rate for Hispanic women.

This racially disparate trend continues at the federal level. In 2000, there were 9,257 women in federal prison. Of these, 3,495 were Black (38 percent) and 5,450 were White (59 percent).[11]

Since 1980, the women's prison population has increased by 500 percent.[12] Since 1990, it has doubled. This exponential rise is largely attributable to a sharp increase in the number of Black female inmates. In 1999, Black women made up almost one-half of all women incarcerated in the United States. Again, this is striking, given that Black women account for only 13.5 percent of the female population in the United States. Overall, they are overrepresented in prison at a rate approximately three times their percentage of the U.S. female population.

The fact that most Black families are headed by women means that the removal of a woman from the home to prison is more likely to have

TABLE 7-6

Lifetime Likelihood of Going to Prison, by Race and Gender, 2001

	Overall	Male	Female
Black	18.6%	32.2%	5.6%
White	3.4%	5.9%	.9%
Hispanic	10%	17.2%	2.2%

Source: U.S. Department of Justice (2003), "Prevalence of Imprisonment in the U.S. Population, 1974–2001," p. 8, Table 9.

a direct effect on children's lives. For 1997, statistics indicate that approximately 70 percent of the women behind bars had children under the age of eighteen. Most had at least two minor children.[13] A look at the figures for women in jail is instructive. Black women are the group most likely to have children (82 percent), followed by Hispanic women (79 percent) and White women (78 percent). The raw numbers reinforce this point. There are 15,854 Black women, 12,290 White women, and 5,789 Hispanic women in jail who have children. Add to this the number of women in prison with children, and the total number of children with mothers tethered to the criminal justice system, in any form, is in the tens of thousands.

Lifetime Likelihood of Going to Prison. In 2003, the Justice Department published a report that calculated the probability, on the basis of race and gender, of going to state or federal prison. The findings, summarized in table 7-6, offer a concise statement of the race and gender disparities in rates of incarceration. There are several notable findings. First, the lifetime likelihood rate of incarceration for Black women, 5.6 percent, is almost as high as the rate for White men, 5.9 percent. Second, the lifetime likelihood of incarceration for Black women is six times higher than the rate for White women (.9 percent). The difference in the chance of incarceration for Black women and for White women is slightly higher than the difference between the chances for Black and White men. Third, Black women have a lifetime incarceration rate that is almost three times the rate for Hispanic women, whose rate is 2.2 percent.[14] Overall, the probability of going to prison for Blacks is almost six times greater than it is for Whites and almost two times greater than it is for Hispanics.

IV. Offending

Offense Patterns. Table 7-7 outlines state-level offending patterns for Black women and for White women. Black women are responsible for approximately one-third of all violent crimes committed by women, while White women account for approximately one-half of these offenses. Specifically, Black women are responsible for 44 percent of all aggravated assaults, and White women account for 43 percent. Black women and White women each account for approximately 42 percent of all robberies. For simple assault, however, there is a wide race differential. In 1998, the percentage for White women (58 percent) was two times higher than the percentage for Black women (30 percent).[15] Racially disparate trends also exist for female murder rates. Black women are responsible for 56 percent of all murders committed by women, while White women are accountable for 43 percent.

Drugs. The justice system's focus on drug-related offenses—the War on Drugs—is largely responsible for the increasing number of Black women in prison. A 1999 report by the Sentencing Project, "Gender and Justice: Women, Drugs and Sentencing Policy," outlines the impact that punitive drug sentencing policies have had on women's incarceration rates.[16] Between 1986 and 1996, almost one-half of the increase in female imprisonment was attributable to drug-related sentences. During the same ten-year period, the number of women imprisoned in state facilities for drug crimes rose by 888 percent. By comparison, the increase in incarceration for nondrug offenses was only 129 percent.

More than two-thirds of the women serving time in federal prison in 2000 had been convicted of a drug offense. For Black women, 66 percent

TABLE 7-7

Offending Patterns for Black and White Women, Select Offenses, 1999

	Black Women	White Women
Violent Crimes Total	33%	50%
Homicide	56%	*
Robbery	42%	42%
Aggravated Assault	44%	43%
Simple Assault	30%	58%

* Information not available

Source: U.S. Department of Justice (1999), "Women Offenders," pp. 2–4.

were serving time for drug offenses (2,317). For White women, 67 percent were serving time for drug offenses (3,559).[17] Many women were sentenced under the federal crack law, which treats possession of crack cocaine—a derivative of powder cocaine—one hundred times more severely than possession of powder cocaine.

The Sentencing Project examined sentencing policies and outcomes in three states—New York, California, and Minnesota—between 1986 and 1995. The study focused on arrest, sentencing, and incarceration data. The review of drug convictions in these states indicated that Black women were disproportionately convicted of drug-related crimes. In New York, for instance, 65 percent of the convictions of Black women were for drug-related offenses.[18] For California, the figure was 39 percent, and for Minnesota, it was 26 percent.[19]

The data on drug use add another dimension to the picture of Black female offenders. Though drug use and drug offending are not the same, studies indicate that most drug users purchase drugs from suppliers who are of their own race.[20] With this in mind, national drug abuse data indicate that there are twice as many White women who use crack as there are Black women who use the drug.[21]

V. Victimization

In addition to their disproportionately high rates of offending, Black women have high rates of victimization. Table 7-8 presents average victimization data for White, Black, American Indian, and Asian women, from 1993 to 1998. These figures include the crimes of rape, sexual assault, robbery, aggravated assault, and simple assault. As indicated, the

TABLE 7-8

Average Annual Victimization Rates for Women,
1993–1998 (per 1,000 ages 12 or older)

	White	Black	American Indian	Asian
Crimes of Violence*	37.6	51.3	96.8	17.4

* Includes rape, sexual assault, and aggravated assault.

Source: U.S. Department of Justice (2001), "Violent Victimization and Race, 1993–98," p. 3, table 2.

TABLE 7-9

Intimate Murder Rates by Gender and Race, 1976–1996 (per 100,000)

	White		Black	
	Male	Female	Male	Female
1976	.89	1.72	16.51	12.01
1981	.92	1.73	11.14	8.40
1986	.70	1.73	7.55	7.19
1991	.53	1.51	5.36	6.58
1996	.36	1.34	2.83	4.51

Source: Bureau of Justice Statistics (1998), "Violence by Intimates: Analysis of Data on Crimes by Current or Former Spouses, Boyfriends, and Girlfriends," p. 40.

rates for Black women (51.3) are almost one-third higher than the rates for White women (37.6) and almost three times higher than the rates for Asian women (17.4). Most notably, however, the rates for American Indian women are approximately *two times* higher than the rates for Black women (96.8).[22]

Murder. Table 7-9 provides trend data (1976–1996) for intimate murder rates. Of all four race and gender groups presented, Black females are most likely to be killed by their intimate partners; their rate is 4.5 per 100,000 people in the population. The rate for Black men is 2.83; for White women, 1.34; and White men, .36. Notably, the rates for all groups have declined sharply in the past two decades. Between 1976 and 1989, more Black men than women were killed by an intimate partner. Since 1990, however, more Black women have been killed by Black male intimates than the reverse.

Other Violence. Table 7-10 provides comparative data on intimate-partner violence for Black and White women, between 1993 and 1998 (per 1,000 people in the population). This includes rape, sexual assault, robbery, aggravated assault, and simple assault. As indicated, for Black and White women, the actual number of assaults declined over the five-year period. Notably, for each year, the rates for Black women are higher than those for White women. Overall, the rate for Black women is 11.2 and the rate for White women is 8.1.

TABLE 7-10

Female Victims of Intimate Partner Violence,[a] per 1,000 (1993–1998)

	White		Black	
	Number	*Rate*	*Number*	*Rate*
1993	895,090	9.8	162,600	11.2
1994	813,670	8.8	174,470	11.9
1995	731,850	7.8	188,510	12.5
1996	689,170	7.3	177,530	13.3
1997	695,930	7.4	129,610	8.9
1998	735,040	7.7	128,660	8.7
Total	4,560,740	8.1	961,380	11.2

[a] Includes rape, sexual assault, robbery, aggravated assault, and simple assault.

Source: U.S. Department of Justice (2001), "Violence Victimization and Race, 1993–1998," p. 9.

VI. *Theory, Anyone?*

Considering the state of affairs regarding research on African American women and crime, it comes as no surprise that there is little theoretical research on Black female offending. Again, the void is noteworthy because Black women are the fastest-growing group within the criminal justice system. Further, they are at the intersection of three forms of marginalization and discrimination—race, gender, and class—referred to as "triple jeopardy."[23] Thus, it could be argued that Black women are a unique empirical class, requiring specially tailored theories.

For the most part, Black women have not been the focal point of criminal justice studies on race or gender; mainstream theories have instead been applied to explain Black women's rates of criminal involvement. When researchers do include them, it is typically through an "add race and stir" approach,[24] wherein theories that have been developed to explain White female offending are, improperly, applied to Black women.[25]

A variety of theories have been offered to understand Black female offending patterns, including theories that consider economic conditions (e.g., employment rates),[26] legislative changes (e.g., welfare laws, three-strikes legislation), and changes in policing strategies (e.g., a shift in focus to nonviolent drug offenses). At the microlevel, psychological explanations have been offered. Though the literature that addresses Black female involvement in the justice system would make for a slim volume, it constitutes an energetic and thoughtful body of research. Four studies with important and interesting theoretical approaches to Black female offenders are discussed here.

Regina Arnold's 1990 study of fifty Black women who were serving time behind bars explores ways in which Black women are treated as deviants prior to their first contact with the criminal justice system.[27] Utilizing interviews, questionnaires, and participant observation, Arnold details the labeling process and how it creates and fosters structural dislocation for Black women. She argues that these labels further marginalize them from three of society's socializing institutions—family, education, and employment. Arnold concludes that Black women's out-group status increases the likelihood that they will become involved in criminal activity. She also observes that there is a direct connection between their experience as crime victims and their involvement as offenders.

In another interesting study, Kathleen Daly examines how race, ethnicity, gender, and family status affect sentencing decisions. Her research, conducted in the 1980s, evaluates how defendants are treated by court officials. Daly conducted interviews with judges, prosecutors, defense attorneys, and probation officers. She also gathered data on criminal defendants. Daly found that offenders, male and female, who had family ties were more likely to receive lenient sentences than other similarly situated offenders who did not have established family bonds. For instance, defendants who were married or had children received less severe sanctions. Daly labels this phenomenon "familial-based sentencing."[28]

A consistent theme in studies of Black women and crime is the link between victimization and the onset of criminal activity. Mary Gilfus's 1992 study supports this connection. Her research is based upon detailed interviews conducted with twenty incarcerated women, Black and White (ages 20 to 41). Three-fourths of the women said they had been physically abused, and more than one-half reported they had been sexually abused. In response to being assaulted, most of the women had run away from home. Noting that running away—a status offense—may be a "sane and logical response,"[29] Gilfus observes, "That logical act of self-protection, however, pushed the young women into finding illegal ways of supporting themselves."[30] To survive, many of the young women engaged in more serious criminal activity, such as prostitution, shoplifting, credit card fraud, and drug-related offending.

In *Compelled to Crime,* Beth Ritchie examines the life histories of battered Black women serving time in jail.[31] Ritchie explores what she labels their "gender entrapment"—a phenomenon that exists "when women who are marginalized in the public sphere because of their race/ethnicity, gender and class and are then battered by their male partners."[32] She completed life-history interviews with thirty-one Black women and six White women. On the basis of these conversations, Ritchie identified several pathways to crime for battered women. These include sex-related crimes (e.g., prostitution); crime committed against men who were not their batterers; crime committed in an attempt to appease their batterer; and drug use as a way to mitigate the physical abuse. On the basis of her findings, Ritchie outlines a gender-entrapment theoretical model that draws from feminist theory, African American feminist approaches to family, and social constructionist approaches.

As indicated by these studies, explanations for Black female offending and how they are processed through the justice system are important issues. This is particularly true since Black women are situated at the crossroads of three critical factors—race, gender, and economics. For these reasons, theoretical analyses should focus squarely on them and not see them only in comparison with other women or with Black men.

VII. Falling into the Gap

The negligible research on Black women, combined with Black women's less-than-positive public representation, may make it more likely that studies about them, when undertaken, are likely to fall into a void. That is, there is no empirical or theoretical language to discuss them as separate and distinct from Black men and White women. The below discussion considers one example of the kind of research that exists within this void.

"Traveling while Black." In March 2000, the Government Accounting Office released a study outlining the race and gender practices of U.S. Customs Service.[33] The study was conducted in response to numerous harassment claims by Black female travelers who had passed through Customs. The report details stops by Customs officials. Of the more than 140 million travelers who entered the United States in 1997 and 1998, approximately 102,000 were detained. The report includes data on the race, gender, and citizenship status of the women stopped and on the type of search that was conducted. Ninety-five percent of the passengers who were stopped (96,900) were subjected to a frisk search. Four percent

(4,080) were strip-searched, and 1 percent (1,020) were subjected to an x-ray screening. Black women were more likely than any other group—including Black men—to be profiled as drug couriers and searched.[34]

The racial disparity was even greater for Black women who were U.S. citizens. They were nine times more likely than White women to be x-rayed following a frisk search.[35] This difference is not explained by the rates at which Customs officials found contraband. The analysis revealed that Black women were less than half as likely to be found carrying contraband as were White women. The report states that Customs has over-hauled its policies and practices, including providing new training for inspectors and supervisors, an enhanced systemized review of complaints, increased emphasis on advisement of passenger rights, and the requirement of supervisory approval for patdown searches.

The degree to which Black women have been singled out by Customs raises the question of whether there are other venues in which they are subjected to racial profiling. While the problem of "driving while Black" has largely been framed as an issue for Black men, it is likely that it is also an issue for Black women. In fact, existing studies indicate that Black women report disproportionately high rates of motorist stops. (See chapter 6 for a detailed discussion of racial profiling.)

The GAO report is one example of the problem created by the absence of a viable literature on Black female offending and victimization. Reports such as this would be categorized under either "racial profiling," which typically focuses on Black men, or under "women," which typically focuses on White women. Neither category, however, acknowledges the unique experiences that Black women have within the justice system.

VIII. Conclusion

This chapter has outlined a range of problems associated with research on Black women and the criminal justice system. One major issue is the availability of statistical data. Another is that Black females are not treated as an empirically viable research topic; they are primarily discussed in connection to Black men or in connection to White women.[36] Simply put, there is no theoretical or empirical location for discussing Black female criminality and victimization. Further, most of the research that does focus on Black women is based on small sample sizes and, therefore, is not generalizable.

This chapter also argues that research on Black women's involvement in the justice system should be placed on the front burner of race and crime research. The current message, which operates as an underground code, is that it is acceptable for African American women to remain invisible. This is problemmatic because in addition to accounting for one-half of the incarcerated female population, they are the fastest-growing race and gender group in the criminal justice system. The barely visible research focus on Black females does not correspond with these figures.

The findings discussed in this chapter are nothing less than a clarion call to devote increased empirical and public attention to Black women and crime. Four recommendations are indicated. First, the Justice Department should publish a comprehensive report focused on African American women and crime. The Justice Department's 1999 study on American Indians and crime provides an excellent model (see chapter 2). The report should be updated every one to two years. Second, more social scientists should develop a research interest in Black women. Leaving this area of research to those most directly affected by it—Black women—is not a workable solution, since Black women make up a small percentage of all academic researchers. Third, once there is increased interest in and scholarship on Black women and crime, there should be at least one criminological journal devoted solely to the issue of African American women and crime. As well, criminology and other social science journals can devote special issues to the topic. Fourth, academic programs, graduate and undergraduate, can develop courses that focus on Black women and crime.

As a race and gender group, Black women have taken a back seat in analyses of the impact of race (where the focus has been on Black men) and in analyses of the impact of gender (where the focus has been on White women). Our collective failure to embrace African American women as a worthwhile area of criminological study can be read many different ways. Most troubling, it may reflect our lack of surprise at the data—which tacitly confirms the view that Black women are expected to be criminals and victims. As more light is shed on their compelling predicament, however, there are fewer and fewer excuses for ignoring them.

8

Race Facts

I. Introduction

In the late 1980s, E. D. Hirsch's book *Cultural Literacy: What Every American Needs to Know* was published. The book's thesis was that, as a group, Americans no longer have knowledge of a basic set of historical, contemporary, and cultural facts. Its index included a list of over five thousand names, phrases, dates, and concepts that, according to the author, all culturally literate citizens should know. The list proved controversial, leading some critics to dismiss it as culturally biased and elitist.

In the race and crime arena there are some indisputable facts. Identifying these facts requires some guidance.[1] In an attempt to promote race and crime literacy, this chapter provides a list of twenty basic race and crime facts. Some facts have been discussed in earlier chapters. For the reader's benefit, references accompany each fact, and, where helpful, tables are included. The list is not intended to be exhaustive, and the facts are not presented in any particular order. The list, offered as a starting point, is designed to address and challenge the prevailing underground codes related to crime and race and encourage foundational literacy.

II. Race Facts

1. There are almost seven million people under the supervision of the criminal justice system. Whites make up 48 percent of those under the control of the criminal justice system; Blacks, 36 percent; Hispanics, 15 percent; and American Indians and Asians, less than 1 percent. Blacks constitute 46 percent of the prison population; Whites, 36 percent; Hispanics, 15 percent; American Indians and Asian Americans together, under 3 percent.

TABLE 8-1

*Number and Percentage of Those in Prison, in Jail,
on Parole, or on Probation, by Race, 2001*

	Prison	Jail	Parole	Probation	Total
White	485,400	260,500	285,500	2,175,600	3,207,000 [48%]
Black	622,200	256,300	299,400	1,228,700	2,406,600 [36%]
Hispanic	209,900	94,100	136,500	469,800	910,300 [15%]
American Indian and	25,200*	10,200*	4,900	29,300	103,800* [less than 1%]
Asian American			4,900	29,300	
Total	1,342,700	621,100	731,200	3,932,700	6,627,700

* Figures include both American Indian and Asian Americans.

Source: U.S. Department of Justice, "Prisoners in 2001" (2002); "Probation and Parole in the United States, 2001" (2002); "Prison and Jail Inmates at Midyear 2000" (2001).

2. Black women's rate of involvement in the criminal justice system (prison, jail, probation, and parole) is increasing faster than that of any other race and gender group, including Black men and White men.

TABLE 8-2

Criminal Justice System Control Rates, , by Race, Ages 20–29 (1989 and 1994).

	1989	1994	% Increase
Males			
White	6.2%	6.7%	8%
Black	23%	30.2%	31%
Hispanic	10.4%	12.3%	18%
Females			
White	1%	1.4%	40%
Black	2.7%	4.8%	78%
Hispanic	1.8%	2.2%	18%

Source: Mauer and Huling (1995), "Young Black Americans and the Criminal Justice System: Five Years Later," table 3.

3. Blacks are more likely than Whites to be rearrested, reconvicted, and returned to prison with a new sentence.

TABLE 8-3

Recidivism Rate for State Prisoners Released in 1994 (Percent of prisoners rearrested, reconvicted, or returned to prison within 3 years of release)

Prisoner Characteristic	Percent of All Released Prisoners	Rearrested	Reconvicted	Returned to Prison with a New Sentence	Returned to Prison without a New Sentence
All Released Prisoners	100%	67.5%	46.9%	25.4%	51.8%
White	50.4%	62.7%	43.3%	22.6%	49.9%
Black	48.5%	72.9%	51.1%	28.5%	54.2%
Other	1.1%	55.2%	34.2%	13.3%	49.5%
Number of Released Prisoners	272,111	272,111	260,226	254,720	227,788

Source: U.S. Department of Justice (2002), "Recidivism of Prisoners Released in 1994," table 8, p. 7.

4. Between 1992 and 1996, American Indians, ages 12 and older had the highest rates of violent victimization (rape, sexual assault, robbery, and assault) of any racial group.

TABLE 8-4

Violent Victimization by Race and Ethnicity, 2000

	Rate, per 1,000 [within each race]
American Indian	52.3
Black	34.1
Hispanic	27.9
White	26.5
Asian	8.4

Source: U.S. Department of Justice (2002), "Hispanic Victims of Violent Crime, 1993–2000," p. 2, table 1.

5. Overall, Black men have the highest homicide victimization rate of any race and gender group. Black men ages 18–24 have the highest rates.

TABLE 8-5

Homicide Victimization Rates, by Race and Gender (ages 18–24), 2000 (per 100,000 in the population)

	Black	White
Male	100	12
Female	13.4	3

Source: U.S. Department of Justice, "Homicide Trends in the U.S.: Age, Gender, and Race Trends."[2]

6. Most crimes involve an offender and a victim of the same race. For example, more than 80 percent of all murders are intraracial.[3]

TABLE 8-6

Murder by Race of Offender and Victim, 2001

	White Offender	Black Offender
White Victim	84%	13%
Black Victim	6%	91%

Source: U.S. Department of Justice (2002), "Crime in the United States 2001," table 2.8.

7. For Black men, the lifetime chance of going to prison is greater than the lifetime chance for any other race and gender group.

TABLE 8-7

Lifetime Likelihood of Going to Prison, by Race and Gender, 2001

	Overall	Male	Female
Black	18.6%	32.2%	5.6%
White	3.4%	5.9%	.9%
Hispanic	10%	17.2%	2.2%

Source: U.S. Department of Justice (2003), "Prevalence of Imprisonment in the U.S. Population, 1974–2001," p. 8, Table 9.

8. More than two-thirds of the people arrested each year are White.

TABLE 8-8

Arrests by Race, 2001 (number and percentage)

	Number	Percentage
White	6,465,887	69.5%
Black	2,617,669	28.1%
American Indian	119,281	1.3%
Asian and Pacific Islander	103,750	1.1%

Source: FBI Uniform Crime Reports (2001), table 43, p. 252.

9. In 2001, Whites made up the majority of the people serving time in federal prison for white-collar offenses. Blacks accounted for 29 percent and Hispanics, 16 percent.

TABLE 8-9

Offense Type, Number, and Percentage of White-Collar Offenders
in Federal Prison, by Race, 2000

Offense Type	White % #	Black % #	Hispanic % #
Fraud	54.1% [3,363]	28.1% [1,746]	12.7% [316]
Embezzlement	56.3% [524]	28.2% [262]	8.4% [78]
Forgery, counterfeiting	42.7% [559]	41.6% [544]	13.2% [173]
Bribery	44.3% [113]	22.4% [57]	21.6% [55]
Tax	71% [542]	11.9% [91]	10.4% [79]
Money laundering	41.1% [405]	13.4% [132]	38.3% [377]
Racketeering, extortion	41.6% [344]	29.2% [241]	18.3% [151]
Gambling, lottery	70.7% [99]	10.1% [10]	14.1% [14]

Source: U.S. Department of Justice (2001), *Sourcebook of Criminal Justice Statistics 2000*, table 5.25, p. 526.[4]

10. The majority of people who use crack cocaine are White. Blacks and Hispanics, however, are disproportionately more likely to use the drug.

TABLE 8-10

Crack Cocaine Use, by Race, 1998

	Total Population	Used within Past Year	Used within Past Month
White	2,870,000	462,000	147,000
Black	1,040,000	324,000	214,000
Hispanic	415,000	157,000	56,000

Source: National Household Survey on Drug Abuse, "Population Estimates 1998," tables 5B–5D.[5]

11. In 1999, Blacks accounted for 85 percent of all convicted crack offenders. This disparity is primarily a result of the federal crack law, which imposes a five-year mandatory minimum sentence for possession of five grams or more of crack cocaine.[6] Under the same law, an offender receives a mandatory sentence of five years for possession of five hundred grams of powder cocaine.

12. In 2000, two-thirds of the White and Black women who were serving time in federal prison had been convicted of a nonviolent drug offense. Overall, 57 percent of the federal prison population is serving time for

nonviolent drug crimes. Between 1998 and 2002, the federal inmate population rose by 31 percent.

TABLE 8-11

Nonviolent Drug Convictions for Federal Prisoners, by Race, 2000

	White	Black
Male	53%	64.4%
Female	67.3%	66.3%

Source: U.S. Department of Justice (2001), *Sourcebook of Criminal Justice Statistics 2000*, tables 6.39, 6.50.

13. In 1999 and 2000, there were more Black men in prisons and jails (791,000) than there were enrolled in institutions of higher learning (603,000).[7]

14. One-third of the Black men ages 20–29 are either in prison, in jail, on probation, or on parole. The control rate for young Black men is more than four times the rate for White men and almost twice that for Hispanic men.

TABLE 8-12

Percentage of Young Men in Criminal Justice System, by Race, 1994

Males	
White	6.7%
Black	30.2%
Hispanic	12.3%

Source: Sentencing Project (1995), "Young Black Americans and the Criminal Justice System: Five Years Later," p. 3.

15. The nation has undergone a major boom in prison construction. It is estimated that during the 1990s, 3,300 prisons were built in the United States. Since 1985, the federal Bureau of Prisons (BOP) has built forty-nine new prisons. In 2002, the BOP was under contract to build thirteen new prisons, which would create approximately fifteen thousand new beds, at a cost of $1.6 billion.[8] States have followed this trend. Between 1990 and 1999, Florida built twenty-seven prisons.[9] Since 1980, California has built twenty-one new prisons, at a cost of $5.3 billion, and has increased its prison population sevenfold.[10]

16. Between 1988 and 1997, the U.S. correctional population grew by more than 60 percent. Two percent of all White adults are under correctional supervision, compared with 9 percent of all Black adults.

TABLE 8-13

Adults under Correctional Supervision, 1988–1997, by Race

	Total	White	Black
1988	3,714,100	2,348,600	1,325,700
1989	4,055,600	2,521,200	1,489,000
1990	4,348,000	2,665,500	1,632,700
1991	4,535,600	2,742,400	1,743,300
1992	4,762,600	2,835,900	1,873,200
1993	4,944,000	2,872,200	2,011,600
1994	5,141,300	3,058,000	2,018,000
1995	5,335,100	3,220,900	2,024,000
1996	5,482,900	3,294,800	2,083,600
1997	5,692,500	3,428,000	2,149,900

Source: U.S. Department of Justice (2001), *Sourcebook of Criminal Justice Statistics 2000*, table 6.2.

17. Despite widespread public fear of crime, between 1992 and 2001, the violent crime rate decreased approximately 33 percent. In the five-year period 1997–2001, the violent crime rate fell by almost 20 percent.[11]

18. Youth of color are disproportionately overrepresented at every stage of the justice system, including referrals, detentions, petitions, waivers to criminal court, and commitments.[12]

19. Felony disenfranchisement—loss of the right to vote because of a felony conviction—disproportionately impacts African American men. Thirteen percent of all African American males (1.4 million men) have lost the right to vote. The rate for Black men is seven times higher than the national average.[13]

20. Whites make up 45 percent of the U.S. death row population; Blacks, 43 percent; and Latinos, 9 percent. Blacks and American Indians are disproportionately overrepresented on death row. Of the offenders who have been executed since 1977, 80 percent had White victims.[14] Studies confirm that race of the victim is the most significant predictor of who

will get the death penalty. Related to this, Blacks who kill Whites are more likely to get the death penalty than anyone else.[15]

TABLE 8-14

Death Row Prisoners, by Race, 2003

	# on Death Row	% of Death Row Inmates
Whites	1,610	45%
Blacks	1,490	43%
Latinos	344	10%
Native Americans	39	1%
Asian Americans	41	1%

Source: NAACP Legal Defense and Educational Fund, "Death Row U.S.A., Spring 2003," p. 1.

This list provides some of the basic facts relating to race, crime, and the criminal justice system. Each one of the facts deserves widespread dissemination and discussion. Though not exhaustive, these twenty facts offer an informational threshold. They are included within the body of knowledge that is minimally required to engage in an informed conversation about race and justice. Hopefully, learning these twenty facts will generate interest in discovering other realities of race and crime.

Afterword

A central argument of this book is that there exist underground codes related to race and crime. These codes operate in two ways. First, they allow us, as a society, to overlook and dismiss nonmainstream populations, such as American Indians and Black women. Second, the codes reinforce stereotypes of crime and criminality, such as how racial profiling is defined, whether police brutality is "a Black thing," and whether certain aspects of the culture (e.g., gangsta rap) are deviant and criminogenic. At their core, the underground codes work to reinforce the dominant paradigm; they determine what is labeled a social problem, appropriate research methods (e.g., examining measured stages of the justice system), and which research questions are accorded prominence. In response to these underground codes, various protective mechanisms have been adopted by marginal populations. Black protectionism is but one example. In sum, the existence of underground codes underscores the need for discussions of what the true and relevant facts are about race and crime.

In one of my favorite quotes, the sociologist C. Wright Mills observes, "All social scientists are, by the fact of their existence, involved in the struggle between enlightenment and obscurantism. In such a world as ours, to practice social science is, first of all to practice the politics of truth."[1] So, we end where we begin, with a lesson from the game of telephone—that we must pay attention, listen with an open and critical ear, and maintain a steadfast interest in the plight of us all.

Notes

NOTES TO CHAPTER I

1. See, e.g., Marjorie Zatz (1987), "The Changing Forms of Racial/Ethnic Biases in Sentencing," *Journal of Research on Crime and Delinquency* 24: 69.

2. See, e.g., Cassia C. Spohn (2000), "Thirty Years of Sentencing Reform: The Quest for a Racially Neutral Sentencing Process," *Policies, Processes and Decisions of the Criminal Justice System,* National Institute of Justice, 429: "The findings of more than 40 years of research examining the effect of race on sentencing have not resolved the issue of whether racial/ethnic minorities are sentenced more harshly than Whites."

3. See, e.g., Dragan Milovanovic & Katheryn K. Russell (eds.) (2001), *Petit Apartheid in the U.S. Criminal Justice System,* Carolina Academic Press.

4. Mainstream analyses are those published in leading criminological journals, such as *Criminology.*

5. Daniel Georges-Abeyie (1990), "The Myth of a Racist Criminal Justice System," in B. MacLean & D. Milovanovic (eds.), *Racism, Empiricism and Criminal Justice,* Collective Press, 11–14.

6. Georges-Abeyie's full description of petit apartheid is:

Does the focus of criminal justice analysis on the formal, easily observed decision-making process obscure or even misdirect attention from the most significant contemporary form of racism within the criminal justice system? [For example] the everyday insults, rough or brutal treatment and unnecessary stops, questions, and searches of blacks; the lack of civility faced by black suspects . . . ; the quality, clarity and objectivity of the judges' instructions to the jury when a black arrestee is on trial; the acceptance of lesser standards of evidence in cases that result in the conviction of black arrestees, as well as numerous other punitively discretionary acts by law enforcement and correctional officers as well a jurists. (*Id.* at 12)

7. See Milovanovic & Russell, *supra* note 3.

8. See, e.g., Donna Bishop & Charles E. Frazier (1996), "Race Effects in Juvenile Justice Decision-Making: Findings of a Statewide Analysis," *Journal of Criminal Law & Criminology* 86(2): 392–414.

9. See, e.g., Sheri Johnson (2001), "Racial Derogation in Prosecutors' Closing Arguments," in Dragan Milovanovic & Katheryn K. Russell (eds.), *Petit Apartheid in the U.S. Criminal Justice System,* 79–102.

10. See, e.g., Ted Chiricos & Charles Crawford (1995), "Race and Imprisonment: A Contextual Assessment of the Evidence," in Darnell Hawkins (ed.), *Ethnicity, Race, and Crime: Perspectives Across Time and Place,* State University of New York Press.

11. Erving Goffman (1973), *The Presentation of Self in Everyday Life,* Overlook Press, 112.

12. *Id.* at 113.

13. Timothy Bynum & Ray Paternoster (1984), "Discrimination Revisited: An Exploration of Front Stage and Backstage Criminal Justice System Decision Making," *Sociology and Social Research* 69: 90, 94.

14. Charles Lawrence III (1987), "The Id, the Ego, and Equal Protection: Reckoning with Unconscious Racism," *Stanford Law Review* 39: 317, 355–358.

15. *Id.*

16. *Id.*

17. 451 U.S. 100 (1981).

18. A. Leon Higginbotham Jr. (1996), *Shades of Freedom: Racial Politics and Presumptions of the American Legal Process,* Oxford University Press, 195.

19. *Id.* at 129 (emphasis added).

20. See Johnson, supra note 9, at 79.

21. *Id.* at 98.

22. *Id.*

23. *Id.* at 60.

24. Donald Black (1989), *Sociological Justice,* Oxford University Press.

25. *Id.* at 4–8.

26. Milovanovic & Russell, *supra* note 3 at xx.

27. 527 U.S. 41 (1999).

28. *Id.* at 45–46.

29. The Gang Violence & Juvenile Crime Prevention Act (2000) (Proposition 21).

30. See generally, Howard Snyder, Melissa Sickmund, & Eileen Poe-Yamagata (2000), *Juvenile Transfers to Criminal Court in the 1990's: Lessons Learned from Four Studies,* Office of Juvenile Justice Delinquency Programs; Sara Raymond (2000) "Comment: From Playpens to Prisons: What the Gang Violence and Juvenile Crime Prevention Act of 1998 Does to California's Juvenile Justice and Reasons to Repeal It," *Golden Gate University Law Review* 30: 223.

31. See Eileen Poe-Yamagata & Michael A. Jones (2000), "And Justice for Some: Different Treatment of Minority Youth in the Justice System," Building Blocks for Youth, 12–13.

32. *Id.* at 14–15.

33. U.S. Sentencing Commission, 2000 *Sourcebook of Federal Sentencing Statistics.*

34. See, e.g., David Baldus, George Woodworth, & Charles Pulaski (1990), *Equal Justice and the Death Penalty: A Legal and Empirical Analysis,* Northeastern University Press.

35. Kristin Schaefer, James Hennessy, & Joseph Ponterotto (2000), "Race as a Variable in Imposing and Carrying Out the Death Penalty in the U.S.," *Journal of Offender Rehabilitation* 30: 35–45.

36. Marc Mauer (1997), "Intended and Unintended Consequences: State Racial Disparities in Imprisonment," The Sentencing Project, 12; The Sentencing Project (2001), *Felony Disenfranchisement Laws in the United States,* www.sentencingproject.org.

37. Government Accounting Office (2000), "U.S. Customs Service: Better Targeting of Airline Passengers for Personal Searches Could Produce Better Results," 2, 10. For a detailed discussion of Black women and the criminal justice system, see chapter 7.

38. *Charleston v. Ferguson,* 532 U.S. 67 (2001).

39. See, e.g., Gregory C. Sisk, Michael Heise, & Andrew Morriss (1998), "Charting the Influences on the Judicial Mind: An Empirical Study of Judicial Reasoning," *New York University Law Review* 73: 1377.

NOTES TO CHAPTER 2

1. For a discussion of "underground codes," see Introduction.

2. U.S. Census Bureau (2002), "The American Indian and Alaska Native Population: 2000" (Census 2000 Brief), table 1, p. 3.

3. "Summary Report, 1995: Doctorate Recipients from United States Universities (Appendix Table A-2)," National Academy of Sciences, www.nsf.gov/sbe/srs/srs00410 [accessed May 6, 2003].

4. It is noted that not all Native Americans are Indian (e.g., Native Hawaiians).

5. U.S. Bureau of Labor Statistics, "A CPS Supplement for Testing Methods of Collecting Racial and Ethnic Information: May 1995" (October 1995).

6. Marianne O. Neilsen & Robert A. Silverman (eds.) (1996) *Native Americans, Crime, and Justice,* Westview Press, 11.

7. Office of Management and Budget, Statistical Directive 15, "Race and Ethnic Standards for Federal Statistics and Administrative Report" (May 12, 1977).

8. Jack Utter (1993), *American Indians: Answers to Today's Questions,* National Woodlands, 11–13; Marianne Neilsen (1994), "Contextualization for

Native American Crime and Criminal Justice System Involvement," in M. Neilsen & R. Silverman (eds.), *Native Americans, Crime and Justice,* 1–12.

9. Utter, *id.,* at 32.

10. The author conducted an annual informal poll of undergraduate students enrolled in "Race, Crime, and Justice," a course at the University of Maryland. Specifically, students were asked to describe how various race and gender groups are portrayed in the mainstream press. For example, they are asked to offer adjectives used to describe "young White male," "young white female," "young Asian male," "young Asian female," "young Black female," "young Black male," "young American Indian male," "young American Indian female," "young Hispanic male," and "young Hispanic female."

11. See, e.g., "Jim Thorpe: All American," in which Burt Lancaster, a White actor, was cast as Jim Thorpe, a stellar American Indian athlete in the first half of the twentieth century.

12. For more information on the AICF, see www.collegefund.org.

13. *New York Times Magazine,* June 21, 1998, 44; June 24, 2001, 12. See also *New York Times Magazine,* November 24, 2002, 26.

14. See, e.g., *The New Yorker,* January 11, 1999, 12.

15. *Honey Magazine,* August 2001, 38. In 2003, the color AICF ad ran in the *New York Times Magazine.* See August 17, 2003, p. 21.

16. See, e.g., Matthew Cella, "Little League Teams Drop Indian Names," *Washington Times,* August 11, 2001, A1: "About 1,500 'offensive' names have been changed across the country under pressure from Indian-advocacy groups."

17. Lanham Act, 15 U.S.C. §1052 (Trademark Act of 1946).

18. "A Public Accommodations Challenge to the Use of Indian Team Names and Mascots in Professional Sports," *Harvard Law Review* (1999) 112: 904–921.

19. Eugene Robinson, "Images, Antics and Insults," *Washington Post Magazine,* August 22, 1999, p. 5. See also Courtland Milloy, "'Redskins' Name as Unbearable as Their Record," *Washington Post,* December 2, 2002, B1.

20. Randall Robinson (2000), *The Debt: What America Owes to Blacks,* Dutton, 91.

21. Jeff Pearlman, "At Full Blast: Shooting Outrageously from the Lip, Braves Closer John Rocker Bangs Away at His Favorite Targets: The Mets, Their Fans, Their City and Just About Everyone in It." December 23, 1999, www.CNNSI.com.

22. *Washington Post,* February 5, 2000, A19.

23. George Orwell (1946), *Animal Farm,* Harcourt, Brace, 112.

24. Eugene Robinson, *supra* note 19.

25. See, e.g., "Short Subjects (Mascot Watch)" *Chronicle of Higher Education* June 8, 2001, A8.

26. See, e.g., Annie Nakao, "N-Word Use Increasing, Not without Protest," *San Francisco Chronicle,* July 29, 2001, A4 (article discusses reactions to Jen-

nifer Lopez's use of the "N word" in the song "I'm Real"). See also Randall Kennedy (2002), *Nigger,* Pantheon, for a detailed legal, historical, and sociological discussion of the "N" word and its uses.

27. Vine Deloria Jr. & Clifford Lytle (1983), *American Indians, American Justice,* University of Texas Press, 161.

28. *Id.* at 162–177.

29. U.S. Department of Justice (1999), "American Indians and Crime," Washington, DC.

30. The rate of interracial victimization is also high for Asian Americans (68 percent). *Id.* (table 9, p. 7).

31. *Id.,* see table 5, p. 4, table 9, p. 7, table 11, p. 9, and table 33, p. 26.

32. U.S. Department of Justice (2001) *Sourcebook of Criminal Justice Statistics 2000,* table 6.35, "Prisoners under Jurisdiction of State and Federal Correctional Authorities," 516.

33. Amy Standefer (1999), "Note: The Federal Juvenile Delinquency Prevention Act: A Disparate Impact on Native American Juveniles," *Minnesota Law Review* 84: 473–503.

34. See, e.g., Standefer, *id.*; R. Bachman, A. Alvarez, & C. Perkins (1996), "Discriminatory Imposition of the Law: Does It Affect Sentencing Outcomes for American Indians?" in Neilsen & Silverman, supra note 6, 197–208; T. Bynum & R. Paternoster (1996), "Discrimination Revisited," in Neilsen & Silverman (eds.), *Native Americans, Crime and Justice,* 228–238; K. Siedschlaw & J. Gilbert (1994), "Native Americans in Criminal Justice," in Hendricks & Byers (eds.), *Multicultural Perspectives in Criminal Justice and Criminology,* Charles C. Thomas, 135–153; David Lester (1999), *Crime and the Native American,* Charles C. Thomas, 154–168.

35. See, e.g., Kim Baca (2001), "The Changing Federal Role in Indian Country," *National Institute of Justice Journal* (April): 9–13.

NOTES TO CHAPTER 3

1. *Jacobellis v. Ohio* 378 U.S. 184, 197 (1964) (Stewart, J., concurring).

2. Amy Binder (1993), "Constructing Racial Rhetoric: Media Depictions of Harm in Heavy Metal and Rap Music," *American Sociological Review* 58 (December): 753–767. See also Tipper Gore (1987), *Raising PG Kids in an X-Rated World,* Abingdon Press.

3. See, e.g., Leola Johnson (1993), "Silencing Gangsta Rap: Class and Race Agendas in the Campaign against Hardcore Rap Lyrics," *Temple Political and Civil Rights Law Review* 3: 25.

4. See, e.g., Theresa Martinez (1997), "Popular Culture as Oppositional Culture; Rap as Resistance," *Sociological Perspectives* 40(2): 265–287.

5. See, e.g., Johnson, *supra* note 3, 29–30.

6. See Kimberlé Williams Crenshaw (1991), "Beyond Racism and Misogyny: Black Feminism and 2 Live Crew," in Mari Matsuda, Charles Lawrence III, Richard Delgado, & Kimberlé Williams Crenshaw (eds.), *Words That Wound,* Westview Press, 111–132; Henry Louis Gates "2 Live Crew Decoded," *New York Times,* June 19, 1990, A23.

7. Johnson, *supra* note 3, 30 fn.18.

8. See, e.g., Carrie Fried (1996), "Bad Rap for Rap: Bias in Reactions to Music Lyrics," *Journal of Applied Social Psychology* 26: 2135–2146.

9. The song "Soulja's Story" appears on *2Pacalypse Now* (1991) (T. Shakur, D. Evans, I. Hayes). See, e.g., Chuck Phillips, "Texas Death Renews Debate over Violent Lyrics," *Los Angeles Times,* September 17, 1992, A1.

10. See also Robert Firester & Kendall T. Jones (2000), "Catchin' the Heat of the Beat: First Amendment Analysis of Music Claimed to Incite Violent Behavior," *Loyola of Los Angeles Entertainment Law Review* 20: 1.

11. See, e.g., Joseph Brean, "Clues Come from Fable, Gangsta Rap," *National Post,* October 25, 2002, A1.

12. See, e.g., Andrew Goldsmith (2002), "Recent Development: Criminal Gang Abatement Act," *Harvard Journal on Legislation* 39: 503.

13. See, e.g., Susan Baker & Tipper Gore (1989), "Some Reasons for 'Wilding,'" *Newsweek,* May 29, 1989, 6–7.

14. www.gallup.com/poll/releases/pr990427.asp.

15. In a 1999 Pew Center Survey, 53 percent of the respondents said that rap music "has been a change for the worse" in the last ten years. Of the choices respondents had, including the Internet, e-mail, gay rights, telemarketing, and cloning, rap music received the highest negative rating. www.pollingreport.com.

16. *Sketches of My Culture* (2001), Artemus Records.

17. Kevin Merida & Hamil Harris, "The Leaders and Their Packs: A Pro Athlete's Entourage of Hangers-On Offers Adulation and Headaches," *Washington Post,* February 21, 2000, C7.

18. See, e.g., Lynne Duke, "The Violent Death of a Peaceful Man; Hip Hop Fans Mourn Slain Rap Pioneer Jam Master Jay of Run-DMC," *Washington Post,* November 1, 2002, C1; Andy Newman & Alan Baker, "Was It a Bad Business Deal or a Music Industry Feud?" *New York Times,* November 1, 2002, B4; *BET Tonight,* November 1, 2002, interview with Russell Simmons (discusses Jason Mizell's life and asserts that the alleged "east coast versus west coast" rap rivalry was instead a conflict of personalities).

19. Subcommittee on Oversight of Government Management, Restructuring, and the District of Columbia of the Committee on Governmental Affairs, United States Senate (1997), "Music Violence: How Does It Affect Our Children," 105th Congress, U.S. Government Printing Office, 31.

20. Subcommittee on Juvenile Justice of the Committee on the Judiciary, United States Senate (1994), "Shaping Our Responses to Violent and Demean-

ing Imagery in Popular Music," 103rd Congress, U.S. Government Printing Office.

21. The final report, a 132-page document, includes a transcript of the hearings, written submissions from the panelists, and statements from a select group of people who did not attend the hearings (e.g., Harry Allen).

22. *Id.* at 9.

23. Basil Talbott, "Moseley-Braun Seeks 'Gangsta Rap' Strategy," *Chicago Sun-Times,* February 24, 1994, 34.

24. U.S. Government Printing Office, *supra,* note 20.

25. "'Shame, Shame' on Time Warner," *Times-Picayune,* May 16, 1997 (wire report).

26. Susan C. Gardstrom (1999), "Music Exposure and Criminal Behavior: Perceptions of Juvenile Offenders," *Journal of Music Therapy* 26(3): 207–221.

27. Stuart Fischoff (1999), "Gangsta' Rap and Murder in Bakersfield," *Journal of Applied Social Psychology* 29: 795–805.

28. Christy Barongan & Gordon Nagayama Hall (1995), "The Influence of Misogynous Rap Music on Sexual Aggression against Women," *Psychology of Women Quarterly* 19(2): 195–207. The researchers do not provide a clear definition of "misogynistic." However, they indicate that pornography is a form of misogyny. They state that "[s]ome musical lyrics express negative and sexist attitudes about woman that are very similar to the messages found in pornographic movies and magazines, including the idea that coercive sexual activity is enjoyable for women" (197).

29. The female participant was a confederate, a member of the research team. *Id* at 200.

30. James Johnson, Lee Jackson, & Leslie Gatto (1995), "Violent Attitudes and Deferred Academic Aspirations: Deleterious Effects of Exposure to Rap Music," *Basic and Applied Social Psychology* 16: 27–41.

31. "Violent" videos were those that included shootings, assaults, or the use of weapons. "Nonviolent" videos were those that focused primarily on dancing and partying. *Id.* at 33–34.

32. Johnson et al., *supra* note 30 at 38.

33. Bruce Wade & Cynthia Thomas-Gunnar (1993), "Explicit Rap Music Lyrics and Attitudes toward Rape: The Perceived Effects on African American College Students' Attitudes," *Challenge: A Journal of Research on African American Men* 4: 51–60.

34. *Id.* at 55.

35. Defined as having a history of "more peer, school, substance abuse, sexual activity, legal, home behavior, and psychiatric problems, and less traditional religious affiliation." Kevin Took & David Weiss (1994), "The Relationship between Heavy Metal and Rap Music and Adolescent Turmoil: Real or Artifact?" *Adolescence* 29: 613, 615.

36. Eminem, a once-reviled White gangsta rapper, has apparently rehabilitated his public image. See, e.g., Frank Rich, "Mr. Ambassador," *New York Times Magazine* (cover story), November 3, 2002, 52; Maureen Dowd "The Boomer's Crooner," *New York Times,* November 24, 2002, 13.

37. See, e.g., Zillmann, D., C. F. Aust, K. D. Hoffman, C. C. Love, V. L. Ordman, J. T. Pop, P. D. Seigler, & R. J. Gibson (1995), "Radical Rap: Does It Further Ethnic Division?" *Basic and Applied Social Psychology* 16: 1–25; Theresa Martinez, *supra* note 4.

38. bell hooks (1994) "Gangsta Culture, Sexism, Misogyny: Who Will Take the Rap?" in hooks, *Outlaw Culture: Resisting Representations* Routledge, 115.

39. *Id.* at 117.

40. Tricia Rose (1994), "Rap Music and the Demonization of Young Black Males," *U.S.A. Today Magazine* 122 (May): 35.

41. Kimberlé Crenshaw (1991), "Mapping the Margins: Intersectionality, Identity Politics, and Violence against Women of Color," *Stanford Law Review* 43 (July): 1241,1289.

42. Binder, *supra* note 2 at 758–760.

43. *Id.* at 760.

44. Fried, *supra* note 8.

45. E-mail received from Carrie Fried, May 7, 2003 (author's file).

46. Public Law 2141.

47. See Johnson, *supra* note 3 at 27.

48. See, e.g., David Segal, "Where's the Return Fire in the Culture Wars?" *Washington Post,* July 2, 2002, C1.

49. Public Enemy (1988), "Don't Believe the Hype," on the compact disk *It Takes a Nation of Millions to Hold Us Back* (Def Jam).

NOTES TO CHAPTER 4

1. See, e.g., "Personal Responsibility and Work Opportunity Reconciliation Act of 1996" (Welfare Reform Bill), P.L. 104-193.

2. See, e.g., "Police Seen Striking a Suspect in Georgia" (Associated Press), *New York Times,* July 14, 2000, A20.

3. In an interesting study of police officer attitudes and perceptions, Abuses of Authority: the National Study of Police Officers' Attitudes (2001), the Justice Department reports that 57 percent of Black officers surveyed agreed (strongly or very strongly) that police are more likely to use physical force against an African American. In contrast, 95 percent of the White officers surveyed stated that they disagreed (strongly or very strongly) that police are more likely to use physical force against African Americans (30–31).

4. See, e.g., Jeffrey Goldberg, "The Color of Suspicion," *New York Times Magazine,* June 20, 1999, 51.

5. See, e.g., Michael Tonry (1995), *Malign Neglect,* Oxford University Press, 50: "Black Americans suffer from what social welfare scholars call 'statistical discrimination,' the attribution to individual persons of characteristics of groups of which they are members."

6. See, e.g., James Q. Wilson (1992), "Race, Crime and Values," *Society.* For a full critique of Wilson's argument, see Katheryn K. Russell (1998), *The Color of Crime,* New York University Press, 124–128.

7. See, e.g., Elisabeth Bumiller, "Mayor Asserts That Grand Jury Blamed Shooting Death on Victim," *New York Times,* March 28, 2001, B4. In March 2003, federal authorities said no civil rights charges would be brought against the police for Dorismond's death. *Washington Post,* March 18, 2003, A9 (wire service).

8. Russell, *supra* note 6 at 34.

9. U.S. Department of Justice (2001), "Contacts between Police and the Public: Findings from the 1999 National Survey," 24.

10. U.S. Department of Justice (2001), "Policing and Homicide, 1976–1998: Justifiable Homicide by Police, Police Officers Murdered by Felons." According to the report, a killing is justified where "it is done to prevent imminent death or serious bodily injury to the officer or another person" (iii).

11. *Id.* at 35.

12. *Id.* at 8–9.

13. *Id.* at 9, 24.

14. The 2002 report, "Law Enforcment Officers Killed and Assaulted," indicates that between 1992 and 2001, 643 officers were killed (83 percent White, 14 percent Black). Fifty-two percent of those who killed law enforcement officers during this period were White, and 39 percent were Black (41, 42).

15. *Id.* at 26. In the discussion on the "felon's criminal record," the study notes that "two thirds . . . had a prior criminal arrest [and that] half were convicted in the past" (26). Both of these statements indicate that a "felon" could be someone who did *not* have a prior conviction.

16. See, e.g., Fox Butterfield, "When the Police Shoot, Who's Counting?" *New York Times,* April, 29, 2001, 5.

17. Jeff Leen, Jo Craven, David Jackson, & Sari Horwitz, "District Police Lead Nation in Shootings," *Washington Post,* November 15, 1998, A1.

18. Title of a 1930s blues classic, written by Andy Razaf, Fats Waller, & Harry Brooks in 1929 and made popular by Louis Armstrong.

19. The historical record indicates that concerns about police use of force against Black citizens are not new. See, e.g., Howard Rabinowitz (1992), "The Conflict between Blacks and the Police in the Urban South, 1865–1900," in Paul Finkelman (ed.), *Race and Criminal Justice,* Garland Press, 318–332.

20. See, e.g., Russell, *supra* note 6.

21. Langston Hughes (1994), *The Return of Simple,* Hill and Wang, 72.

22. Malcolm D. Holmes (2000), "Minority Threat and Police Brutality: Determinants of Civil Rights Criminal Complaints in U.S. Municipalities," *Criminology* 38(2): 343–367.

23. *Id.*

24. *Id.* at 350 (citations omitted).

25. PBA poster observed on the R train in Manhattan, New York (October 1, 2000).

26. *Nightline,* ABC television network, July 13, 2000. Sgt. Preston Gilstrap, of Texas, was a panelist on the show, which was devoted to discussing a case involving the beating of a Black man, Thomas Jones, by Philadelphia police officers.

27. See, e.g., *Chicago v. Morales,* 527 U.S. 41 (1999).

28. Randall Kennedy, "Suspect Policy," *The New Republic* 34 (September 13 & 20, 1999), 30–35.

NOTES TO CHAPTER 5

1. *Washington Journal,* C-Span, April 1, 2001 (comment by a self-identified African American caller).

2. See Katheryn K. Russell (1998), *The Color of Crime,* New York University Press, 56–65.

3. John Kitsuse & Malcolm Spector (1972), "Toward a Sociology of Social Problems: Social Conditions, Value Judgments, and Social Problems," *Sociology of Social Problems* 20: 407, 415.

4. Theodore Sasson (1995), "African American Conspiracy Theories and the Social Construction of Crime," *Sociological Inquiry* 65: 265–285.

5. Regina Austin (1995), "Beyond Black Demons & White Devils: Anti-Black Conspiracy Theorizing & the Black Public Sphere," *Florida State University Law Review* 22: 1021, 1032–1033.

6. Douglas Massey & Nancy Denton (1993), *American Apartheid,* Harvard University Press, 74–75.

7. See, e.g., Eric Schmitt, "Analysis of Census Finds Segregation along with Diversity," *New York Times,* April 4, 2001, A15.

8. Black protectionism operates at the local level (see, e.g., Jim Herron Zamora, "Black Muslim Leader Arrested," *San Francisco Chronicle,* September 20, 2003, A25, for a discussion of Oakland's response to a rape case against a local Muslim leader, Yusef Bey). The focus of this chapter, however, is on outlining national instances to which it applies.

9. See, e.g., Kevin Sack, "Pressed against a 'Race Ceiling,'" *New York Times,* April 5, 2001, A12.

10. See, e.g., Joe Davidson (1996), "Targets for Scrutiny," *Emerge Magazine* (October 1996): 38–42 [discussion of charges against Harlem Congressman

Adam Clayton Powell, Jr. and reference a *Washington Post* study that found that Blacks made up 14 percent of the targets of the 465 political corruption investigations launched from 1983 to 1988 (at a time when Blacks constituted only 3 percent of officeholders)].

11. See, e.g., Ward Churchill & Jim Vander Wall (1990), *The COINTEL-PRO Papers,* South End Press.

12. www.rainbowpush.org.

13. A January 24–25, 2001, Fox News/Opinion Dynamics poll reported that 63 percent of Blacks surveyed held a "favorable" opinion of Jesse Jackson, compared with 24 percent of Whites.

14. See, e.g., Debra Mathis, "The Clinton Legacy and Black America," Savoy *Magazine,* February 2001, 70 (article features a computer-enhanced photograph of a "Black" Bill Clinton).

15. Toni Morrison, "Talk of the Town," *The New Yorker,* October 5, 1998, 31–32.

16. Darryl Fears, "Bill Clinton, Soul Brother? Honor Raises Some Eyebrows," *Washington Post,* October 19, 2002, C1.

17. See, e.g., Kate Hann "Three Penn Experts Explore the Ways Politics and the Press Affect Each Other," May 26, 1994, www.upenn.edu/pennnews/current/features/199/052694/press-forum.html.

18. Leigh Hopper, "'Can't Put the Genie Back': Past Controversies Don't Daunt Joycelyn Elders, Who Speaks Here Today," *Houston Chronicle,* December 1, 2000, A37.

19. This example is based upon the author's conversation with Ronald Walters, professor of government and politics at the University of Maryland (June 2001).

20. See, e.g., Barbara Kopple's documentary *Fallen Champ: The Untold Story of Mike Tyson* (1993). One scene shows Minister Louis Farrakhan, leader of the Nation of Islam, at a pro-Tyson rally. Alluding to Desiree Washington, he lectures women on the "damned deceitful games you play."

21. For a discussion of the Black community's conflicted response to Tyson, see, e.g., Clarence Page, "Hey Give Him a Break," *Baltimore Sun,* June 27, 1995, 11A.

22. See, e.g., Larry Hugick, "Opinion on Thomas Shifted as Hearings Progressed," *Gallup Poll Monthly,* October 1991, shows that, following the sexual harassment charges, Black support for Thomas increased from 54 percent to 67 percent; see also Louis Harris, "Thomas Tactics Work: Coalition of Blacks and Conservatives Offsets Losses among Women," The Harris Poll (1991): "By claiming that he was the victim of an organized effort to depict him as a stereotype of black male sexual excesses and that the hearings were directed at him because of his race, Thomas was able to increase black support for him from 58-34 to 65-32." October 15, 1991, Creators Syndicate, Inc.

23. See, e.g., Patricia Hill Collins (1998), *Fighting Words: Black Women and the Search for Justice,* University of Minnesota Press, 201–203 (discussion of "standpoint" theory and racial solidarity).

24. Jenee Osterheldt, "Does Thug Deserve a Hug? R. Kelly Fans Unsure," *Milwaukee Journal-Sentinel,* July 28, 2002, 8B.

25. See, e.g., Ana Mendieta, "Most Say Radio Should Pull Plug," *Chicago Sun-Times,* June 6, 2002, 8 (poll found that 56 percent of those surveyed believed that, in light of child pornography allegations against R. Kelly, radio stations should stop playing his music. The poll does not provide a breakdown of responses based on the race of those who participated in the poll); Stephen A. Crockett Jr., "R. Kelly Fans Separate the Sound from the Furor," *Washington Post,* January 25, 2003, C1 (discussion of Black radio listeners' reactions to new child pornography charges filed against R. Kelly in January 2003).

26. For related article, see Adam Shatz, "About Face," *New York Times Magazine,* January 20, 2002, 18, which spotlights Glen Loury's political return home to liberal politics and the Black community.

27. See, e.g., Michael Powell, "Two Sides of Ex-NBA Star Clash in Shooting Death," *Washington Post,* March 1, 2002, A1. For a critique of Williams's actions, see Roy S. Johnson, "When Good Men Go Bad," *Savoy Magazine,* August 2002, 18.

28. Regina Austin (1992), "'The Black Community,' Its Lawbreakers, and a Politics of Identification," *Southern California Law Review* 65: 1769, 1772.

29. See, e.g., Tracy Thompson & Elsa Walsh, "Jurors View Videotape of Barry Drug Arrest," *Washington Post,* June 29, 1990, A1.

30. Jill Nelson, "We've Been Bill-boozled," *Savoy Magazine,* May 2001, 46, 48.

31. See, e.g., John Braithwaite (1989), *Crime, Shame and Reintegration,* Cambridge University Press.

32. In a comedy sketch on O. J. Simpson, Chris Rock questions why so many Black people were excited about the Simpson acquittal. "Black people too happy, White people too mad. White people are like, 'man, this is bullshit.' I ain't seen White people that mad since they canceled M*A*S*H. Black people are like, 'Yeah, we won!' What the fuck did we win? Every day I look in my mailbox for my O. J. prize—nothin'!" Chris Rock (1997), "Roll with the New," Dreamworks Records.

33. See, e.g., *Hudson v. MacMillan* 503 U.S. 1 (1992), *Adarand Constructors, Inc. v. Pena* 515 U.S. 200 (1995).

34. During Clinton's presidency, the incarceration rates rose to peak levels, leading some to refer to him as the "incarceration president" (see Justice Policy Institute, "Too Little, Too Late: President Clinton's Legacy," www.cjcj.org).

35. Randall Robinson (2000), *The Debt: What America Owes to Blacks,* Dutton, 101.

36. Some have questioned the sincerity of Clinton's affection for African Americans. Dick Morris, a former Clinton adviser, stated that Clinton's embrace of the Black community was both sincere and opportunistic. According to Morris, Clinton knew that if he ever got into legal trouble that was prosecuted in court, the trial would be held in the District of Columbia. Given the city's racial composition (approximately 60 percent African American), Clinton predicted that he would have at least one Black juror and therefore get at least a hung jury ("Judith Regan Tonight," interview with Dick Morris, Fox Television News, April 21, 2001).

37. For a more detailed discussion of Black and White opinion in the Simpson case, see Russell, *supra* note 2 at 47–68.

NOTES TO CHAPTER 6

1. See, e.g., Katheryn K. Russell (1998) *The Color of Crime,* 36–38.

2. 517 U.S. 806 (1996).

3. David Harris (2002) describes the DWB label as a "cynical twist on the offense of driving while intoxicated." *Profiles in Injustice,* New Press, 129.

4. During this period, some criminological writings focused on the "informal" stages of the justice system. See, e.g., Daniel Georges-Abeyie (1990) "The Myth of a Racist Criminal Justice System?" in B. MacLean & D. Milovanovic (eds.), *Racism, Empiricism and Criminal Justice,* Collective Press; Dragan Milovanovic & Katheryn K. Russell (eds.) (2001), *Petit Apartheid in the U.S. Criminal Justice System* (see chapter 1 for a detailed discussion of the informal stages).

5. Discussion based on author's correspondence with David Harris, professor of law at the University of Toledo (on file with author).

6. *U.S. v. Brignoni-Ponce,* 422 U.S. 873 (1975).

7. See, e.g., "4 Ex-Officers in Ala. Admit Extorting Money from Hispanic Motorists, Others," *Washington Post* ("Nation in Brief"), June 24, 2001, A10.

8. See, e.g., Kevin R. Johnson (2000), "The Case against Race Profiling in Immigration Enforcement," *Washington University Law Quarterly* 78(3): 675, 692–702; Leonel Sanchez, "Latinos Protest Ethnic Profiling: Complaints Mount against Immigration and Police Officers," *San Diego Union-Tribune,* July 24, 2000, A1; John Cloud, "What's Race Got to Do with It?" *Time,* July 30, 2001, www.time.com/time. For a discussion of racial profiling and American Indians, see, e.g., L. M. Silko (1996) *Yellow Woman and a Beauty of the Spirit: Essays on Native American Life Today,* Simon & Schuster, 107–123.

9. For instances of gang-related profiling of Asian Americans, see, e.g., David Harris, *supra* note 3 at 6–8, 135–139.

10. CNN/*USA Today* Gallup poll, September 14–15, 2001. Question 41: "Please tell me if you would favor or oppose . . . requiring Arabs, including those who are U.S. citizens, to undergo special, more intensive security checks before

boarding airplanes in the U.S." See also Catherine Donaldson Evans, "Terror Probe Changes Face of Racial Profiling Debate," October 1, 2001, www. foxnews.com.

11. See also "Traffic Stops along the Border Statistics Study Act of 2001" May 9, 2001, H.R. 1778.

12. For a detailed and up-to-date catalog of racial profiling legislation, see www.profiliesininjustice.com.

13. For a detailed discussion of pretext, see *Whren v. United States,* 517 U.S. 806 (1996).

14. Missouri Revised Statutes, Chapter 590 (August 28, 2001).

15. U.S. Department of Justice-CRS, "Agreement between St. Paul Police Department and St. Paul Chapter of the NAACP" (2001).

16. *Ledford v. City of Highland Park,* 2000 U.S. Dist. LEXIS 11101 (N.D. Ill. October 5, 2000); *Chavez v. Illinois State Police,* 251 F.3d 612 (2001).

17. Consent Decree, p. 5.

18. 517 U.S. 456 (1996).

19. *Id.* at 639.

20. HR. 2074, S. 989 (2001).

21. *Wilkins v. Maryland State Police,* Civil No. MJG-93-468 (D.Md. 1996). See Laura Barnhardt, "State Settles Bias Case: Board OKs Agreement in Racial Profiling Suit," *Baltimore Sun,* April 3, 2003, 1B (discussion of Maryland troopers' settlement. Among other items, the agreement requires that troopers videotape traffic stops and provide motorists with a brochure on the procedure for filing a racial profiling claim.).

22. "Plaintiff's Fourth Monitoring Report: Pedestrian and Car Stop Audit, Philadelphia Office of the American Civil Liberties Union," July 1998.

23. New Jersey Department of Law and Public Safety (April 1999), "Interim Report of the State Police Review Team Regarding Allegations of Racial Profiling," www.state.nj.us/lps.

24. The report concludes that some New Jersey state troopers were intentionally falsifying data on their vehicle stop reports. The review found that some officers were engaged in racial profiling against minority motorists. To obscure their practices, these officers used data gathered on White motorists for their written reports on stops involving Black motorists. In April 1999, indictments were issued against two members of the New Jersey State Police. See, e.g., David Kocieniewski, "Trenton Charges 2 Troopers with Faking Drivers' Race," *New York Times,* April 20, 1999, A23.

25. Richard Morin, "The Latest on DWB," *Washington Post,* February 16, 2003, B5 (based on research by Richard Lundman and Robert Kaufman).

26. For a discussion of other manifestations of living while Black, see generally Kenneth Meeks (2000), *Driving while Black: Highways, Shopping Malls,*

Taxicabs, Sidewalks, Broadway Books; see also Jabari Asim (2001), *Not Guilty: Twelve Black Men Speak Out on Law, Justice and Life,* Amistad Books.

27. Bryonn Bain (2000), "Walking while Black," *Village Voice,* April 26–May 2, 2000, www.villagevoice.com/issues/0017. Bain was also interviewed by Mike Wallace for an installment of *60 Minutes,* which aired February 11, 2001. Five months following the incident, and four court appearances later, all charges were dropped against Bain and his two relatives, Kristofer Bain and Kyle Vazquez.

28. *Id.*

29. Paul Butler, "'Walking while Black': Encounters with the Police on My Street," *Legal Times,* November 10, 1997, 23.

30. 527 U.S. 41 (1999).

31. Chicago, IL, Municipal Code Section 8-4-015 (1992).

32. See, e.g., Stuart Taylor, "Cabbies, Cops, Pizza Deliveries and Racial Profiling," *National Journal,* June 17, 2000, 1891; Meeks, *supra* note 26 at 218–220.

33. Alonzo Jackson was awarded $850,000 ($350,000 compensatory and $500,000 punitive damages), and the other young men were awarded $75,000 apiece ($25,000 compensatory and $50,000 punitive damages). *Alonzo Jackson & Rasheed Plummer v. Eddie Bauer,* Case No. AW-96-54, December 11, 1995 (complaint). See also Joann Loviglio, "Civil Rights Not Violated, But Eddie Bauer Told to Pay $1 Million in Shoplifting Case," *Legal Intelligencer,* October 10, 1997, 4. For another incident of "consumer racism" see Steven Holmes, "Large Damage Award to Black Whom Store Suspected of Theft," *New York Times,* December 11, 1997, A17. See also Neely Tucker, "Two Allege Bias at Store in Georgetown: Black Women Sue after Being Barred from Clothes Shop," *Washington Post,* December 12, 2002, B3.

34. 528 U.S. 119 (2000).

35. See, e.g., *Washington Post,* December 13, 2002, A38 ("Nation in Brief") (Federal government closed the investigation into the shooting, finding insufficient evidence to support criminal charges against the four officers); Lisa O'Neill & Michael Fisher, "Officers Don't Face Charges: Tyisha Miller: The Justice Department Says Evidence Is Lacking in the 4-Year-Old Fatal Shooting," *Press Enterprise,* December 13, 2002, A1.

36. 195 F.3d 111 (2d Cir. 1999).

37. *Brown v. City of Oneonta,* 221 F.3d 329 (2d Circuit 1999), *cert. denied,* 122 S.Ct. 44 (2001). Notably, two of the African American opinion/editorial columnists at the *Washington Post* and the *New York Times,* William Raspberry and Bob Herbert, respectively, wrote about the case. Their columns, which were published approximately one month apart, were both titled, "Breathing while Black." See Bob Herbert, "Breathing while Black," *New York Times,* November

4, 1999, A27; William Raspberry, "'Breathing while Black,'" *Washington Post* December 6, 1999, A27.

38. See, e.g., Gregory Kane, "Writer, NAACP Owed Credit for Righting Texas Injustice," *Baltimore Sun*, April 12, 2003, 1B; Paul Duggan, "Massive Drug Sweep Divides Texas Town," *Washington Post*, January 22, 2002; Jennifer Gonnerman, "Tulia Blues," *Village Voice*, August 1–7, 2001. In August 2003, Texas Governor Rick Perry pardoned thirty-five people who were convicted in the sting. Another form of racial profiling, which falls within the Living While Black category, is name profiling. A 2002 study by professors Marianne Bertrand and Sendhil Mullainathan indicates that job applicants who have "Black-sounding" names (e.g., Tamika, Ebony, Tyrone) are more likely to be discriminated against in the job market than are those with "White-sounding" names (e.g., Neil, Greg, Emily, Jill). See, e.g., Associated Press, "Looking for Work? Using 'White' Name Helps Out," *Seattle Times*, A4.

39. Steven D. Levitt & John J. Donohue (2001), "The Impact of Legalized Abortion on Crime," *Quarterly Journal of Economics* 116: 379–420.

40. *Id.*

41. *Id.*

42. See, e.g., Philip Cook & John Laub (2002), "After the Epidemic: Recent Trends in Youth Violence in the United States," *Crime and Justice*, 1.

43. Karen Brandon, "Legalized Abortions Linked to Drop in Crime," *Ottawa Citizen*, August 10, 1999, A1.

44. Michael Tonry (1995), *Malign Neglect: Race, Crime and Punishment in America*, Oxford University Press.

45. *Ferguson v. Charleston,* 532 U.S. 67 (2001).

46. See, e.g., Tatsha Robertson, "3 N.H. Addicts Give Up Fertility; Pick Controversial Program Offering $200," *Boston Globe*, August 28, 1999, B1; Pam Bailiwick, "Cash-for-Sterilization Plan Draws Addicts and Critics," *New York Times,* July 14, 1999, A7.

47. Avram Goldstein, "Group to Pay Addicts to Take Birth Control," *Washington Post,* June 26, 2000, B1.

48. 31 F.Supp. 2d 23 (1998).

49. *Id.* at 29–30.

50. See, e.g., "Judge Is Forced to Lengthen Sentences for Crack," *New York Times,* November 27, 1995, B5; Russell, *supra* note 1 at 133 & 188, n.6.

51. Harris, *supra* note 3 at 98. See also Russell, *supra* note 1 at 34 (discussion of "protective mechanisms" employed by Black men to avoid profiling); "ABC, Racial Profiling and Law Enforcement: America in Black and White" (2000), videotape.

NOTES TO CHAPTER 7

1. Feminist scholar bell hooks (1981) offers an incisive historical critique of the portrayal of Black women and how history influences contemporary representations: *Ain't I a Woman: Black Women and Feminism,* South End Press, 51–86.

2. Dana Britton (2000), "Feminism in Criminology: Engendering the Outlaw," *American Academy of Political and Social Science* 571 (September 2000): 57, 58.

3. Kimberlé Crenshaw (1991), "Mapping the Margins: Intersectionality, Identity Politics, and Violence against Women of Color," *Stanford Law Review* 43: 1241–1299.

4. See, e.g., *The Sourcebook* (an annual Bureau of Justice Statistics publication, hereafter, *The Sourcebook*); "Women Offenders" (Lawrence Greenfield & Tracy Snell, December 1999); data from the National Incident-Based Reporting System (NIBRS), Prosecution of Federal Arrests (PFA); Offender-Based Transaction Statistics (OBTS); National Judicial Reporting Program (NJRP); and the National Pre-Trial Reporting Program (NPRP).

5. See, e.g., U.S. Department of Justice (1994), "Young Black Male Victims" (December 1994); Marc Mauer & Tracy Huling (1995), "African Americans and the Criminal Justice System, Five Years Later," Sentencing Project (report focuses primarily upon the impact of the criminal justice system on Black men).

6. Lawrence Greenfeld, at the Bureau of Justice Statistics, graciously and patiently spent time locating and putting together statistics on Black women in the justice system.

7. See, e.g., U.S. Census Bureau, Census 2000 Summary File 1, "Female Population by Race Alone or in Combination and Age for the United States: 2000, Table 6 (Internet release date, October 3, 2001); *Id.,* "Total Population by Age, Race and Hispanic or Latino Origin for the United States: 2000 (Table 1)," February 14, 2000, www.census.gov.

8. Mauer & Huling, *supra* note 5.

9. See, e.g., Government Accounting Office (1999), "Women in Prison: Issues and Challenges Confronting U.S. Correctional Systems," 28, table 111.5.

10. This table includes data for sentenced inmates only. A more comprehensive look would include data on inmates in jails. In fact, the statistics on females in prisons and jails show that Black women make up 45 percent of the population; White women, 36 percent; Hispanic women, 16 percent; and "Other" women (American Indians and Asians), 3 percent. U.S. Department of Justice (2000), "Prison and Jail Inmates Midyear 1999," 10, table 12.

11. *The Sourcebook,* 526, table 6.50.

12. Government Accounting Office (1999), "Women in Prison: Issues and Challenges Confronting U.S. Correctional Systems," GAO/GGD-00-22 AO, 2.

13. *Id.* at 31, table III.8.

14. U.S. Department of Justice (1997), "Lifetime Likelihood of Going to State or Federal Prison," Bureau of Justice Statistics, NCJ 160092.

15. U.S. Department of Justice (1999), "Women Offenders," NCJ 175688, 2.

16. Marc Mauer, Cathy Potler, & Richard Wolf, Sentencing Project, November 1999.

17. *Sourcebook, supra* note 4, 526, table 6.50.

18. Mauer et al., *supra* note 16, 10.

19. *Id.* at 14.

20. See, e.g., Jack Riley (1997), "Crack, Powder Cocaine, and Heroin: Drug Purchase and Use Patterns in Six U.S. Cities," National Institute of Justice, 1 (survey respondents were most likely to report that their main supplier was from their same racial or ethnic background).

21. Department of Health and Human Services (1997), "National Household Survey on Drug Abuse: Population Estimates 1996," tables 5A–5D.

22. U.S. Department of Justice (2001), "Violent Victimization and Race, 1993–98," 3, table 3.

23. Regina Arnold (1990), "Women of Color: Processes of Victimization and Criminalization of Black Women," *Social Justice* 17(3): 153, 163.

24. Sally S. Simpson (1999), "Feminist Theory, Crime, and Justice," *Criminology* 27: 605, 619.

25. Simpson describes this as a "shortsightedness that pervades feminist thinking." *Id.*

26. See, e.g., Gary Hill & Elizabeth M. Crawford (1990), "Women, Race, and Crime," *Criminology* 28(4): 601–626.

27. *Id.*

28. Kathleen Daly (1989), "Neither Conflict nor Labeling nor Paternalism Will Suffice: Intersections of Race, Ethnicity, Gender, and Family in Criminal Court Decisions," *Crime & Delinquency* 35(1): 136–168.

29. Mary Gilfus (1992), "From Victims to Survivors to Offenders: Women's Routes of Entry and Immersion into Street Crime," *Women & Criminal Justice* 4(1): 63, 77.

30. *Id.*

31. Beth Ritchie (1996), *Compelled to Crime: The Gender Entrapment of Battered Black Women,* Routledge.

32. *Id.* at 133.

33. Government Accounting Office (2000), "U.S. Customs Service: Better Targeting of Airline Passengers for Personal Searches Could Produce Better Results" (hereafter "GAO Report"), http://www.access.gao.gov.

34. Stephen Barr, "Study Finds Wide Disparities in Customs' Intrusive Searches," *Washington Post,* April 10, 2000, A1.

35. GAO Report, *supra* note 33 at 10.

36. Kerry Carrington (1993) comments that old paradigms, such as those focusing on White women, reinforce the centrality of gender. In her analyses of the treatment of Aboriginal girls, Carrington notes, "Even where concerns about the specificity of black women have been considered in feminist discourses the issue has tended to be dealt with by simply adding one essentialism onto another, that is: racism + sexism = black women = white women only more so." *Offending Girls,* 17 [citations omitted].

NOTES TO CHAPTER 8

1. As one step in this direction, Gregg Barak (1991) compiled a list of multicultural readings "essential for understanding the African-American experience in relationship to crime control and justice" (184). "Cultural Literacy and the Multicultural Inquiry into the Study of Crime and Justice," *Journal of Criminal Justice* 2(2): 173–192.

2. www.ojp.usdoj.gov/bjs.

3. In stark contrast to the general rule, it is noted that 70 percent of all crimes committed against American Indians are interracial. U.S. Department of Justice (1999), "American Indians and Crime," 7, table 9.

4. www.albany.edu/sourcebook.

5. www.samhsa.gov.

6. U.S. Department of Justice (2002) "Federal Cocaine Offenses: An Analysis of Crack and Powder Penalties." (The report states, "Reductions in crack offenses would primarily affect Black defendants. Based on FY 1999 data, the Sentencing Commission estimates that if crack mandatory minimum triggers were moved from five grams to 20 grams, 85.6% of defendants affected by the change would be Black." 28.)

7. Justice Policy Institute (2002), "Cellblocks or Classrooms? The Funding of Higher Education and Corrections and Its Impact on African American Men," National Summary-Fact Sheet, www.justicepolicy.org.

8. U.S. Department of Justice (2002), "Federal Bureau of Prisons Management of Construction Contracts," Report No. 02-32.

9. Summary of Florida State Correctional Facilities (June 30, 2001), www.dc.state.fl.us.

10. Vince Beiser, "How We Got to Two Million," *Mother Jones,* July 10, 2001. See also Fox Butterfield, "Study Shows Building Prisons Did Not Prevent Repeat Crimes," *New York Times,* June 3, 2002, A11.

11. U.S. Department of Justice (2002), "Crime in the United States, 2001," 64, table 1. See also U.S. Department of Justice (2002), "Criminal Victimization 2001: Changes 2000–01 with Trends 1993–2001," 2.

12. Eileen Poe-Yamagata (2000), "And Justice for Some," Building Blocks for Youth." See also Joan McCord, Cathy Spatz Widom, & Nancy Crowell

(eds.) (2001), *Juvenile Crime, Juvenile Justice,* National Academies Press, 228–259; Mike Males & Dan Macallair (2000), "The Color of Justice: An Analysis of Juvenile Adult Court Transfers in California," American Bar Association & National Bar Association; "Justice by Gender: The Lack of Appropriate Prevention, Diversion and Treatment Alternatives for Girls in the Justice System" (2001) (reports that delinquency cases involving Black girls increased by 106 percent between 1985 and 1994, compared with an increase of 83 percent for all girls).

13. The Sentencing Project (2001), "Felony Disenfranchisement Law in the United States."

14. NAACP Legal Defense and Educational Fund (January 2003), "Death Row USA," www.deathpenaltyinfo.org.

15. See, e.g., Raymond Paternoster (2003), "An Empirical Analysis of Maryland's Death Sentencing with Respect to the Influence of Race and Legal Jurisdiction." Released January 7, 2003, www.urhome.umd.edu/newsdesk/pdf/exec.pdf (Executive Summary).

NOTE TO THE AFTERWORD

1. C. Wright Mills (1959), *The Sociological Imagination,* Oxford University Press, 178.

Bibliography

Andersen, Margaret L., & Patricia Hill Collins (2001). *Race, Class and Gender: An Anthology.* Belmont, CA: Wadsworth.

Arnold, Regina A. (1990). "Women of Color: Processes of Victimization and Criminalization of Black Women." *Social Justice* 17(3): 153–166.

Asim, Jabari, ed. (2001). *Not Guilty: Twelve Black Men Speak Out on Law, Justice and Life.* New York: Amistad.

Austin, Regina (1995). "Beyond Black Demons & White Devils: Anti-Black Conspiracy Theorizing & the Black Public Sphere," *Florida State University Law Review* 22: 1021.

——— (1992). "'The Black Community,' Its Law Breakers, and a Politics of Identification," *Southern California Law Review* 65: 1769.

Bain, Bryonn (2000). "Walking while Black," *The Village Voice,* April 26–May 2, 2000, www.villagevoice.com/issues/0017/bain.

Baskin, Deborah R., & Ira B. Sommers (1998). *Casualties of Community Disorder.* Boulder, CO: Westview Press.

Binder, Amy (1993). "Constructing Racial Rhetoric: Media Depictions of Harm in Heavy Metal and Rap Music," *American Sociological Review* 58: 753–767.

Black, Donald (1989). *Sociological Justice.* New York: Oxford University Press.

Blumstein, Alfred (1993). "Racial Disproportionality of U.S. Prison Populations Revisited," *University of Colorado Law Review* 64: 743.

Britton, Dana (2000). "Feminism in Criminology: Engendering The Outlaw," *Annals of the American Academy of Political and Social Science* 571: 57.

Bushway, Shawn, & Anne Morrison Piehl (2001). "Judging Judicial Discretion: Legal Factors and Racial Discrimination in Sentencing," *Law & Society Review* 35(4): 733–764.

Bynum, Tim, & Ray Paternoster (1984). "Discrimination Revisited: An Exploration of Front and Backstage Criminal Justice Decision Making," *Sociology and Social Research* 69: 90–108.

Carrington, Kerry (1993). *Offending Girls: Sex, Youth and Justice.* Sydney, New South Wales, Australia: Allen & Unwin.

Chesney-Lind, Meda (1989). "Girl's Time and Woman's Place: Toward a Feminist Model of Female Delinquency," *Crime and Delinquency* 35: 5–29.

Cole, David (1999). *No Equal Justice: Race and Class in the American Criminal Justice System*. New York: New Press.

Collins, Catherine (1997). *The Imprisonment of African American Women*. Jefferson, NC: McFarland.

Collins, Patricia Hill (1998). *Fighting Words: Black Women & the Search for Justice*. Minneapolis: University of Minnesota Press.

Crenshaw, Kimberlé (1993). "Beyond Racism and Misogyny: Black Feminism and 2 Live Crew." In M. Matsuda, C. Lawrence, R. Delgado, & K. Crenshaw (eds.), *Words That Wound*. Boulder, CO: Westview Press, 111–132.

——— (1991). "Mapping the Margins: Intersectionality, Identity Politics, and Violence against Women of Color," *Stanford Law Review* 43: 1241–1299.

Daly, Kathleen (1989). "Neither Conflict nor Labeling nor Paternalism Will Suffice: Intersections of Race, Ethnicity, Gender, and Family in Criminal Court Decisions," *Crime and Delinquency* 35(1): 136–168.

Daly, Kathleen, & Lisa Maher (1998). "Crossroads and Intersections: Building from Feminist Critique." In K. Daly & L. Maher (eds.), *Criminology at the Crossroads*. New York: Oxford University Press.

Davis, Angela J. (2002). "Incarceration and the Imbalance of Power." In Marc Mauer & Meda Chesney-Lind (eds.), *Invisible Punishment: The Collateral Consequences of Mass Incarceration*. New York: New Press, 61–78.

Deloria, Vine, & Clifford M. Lytle (1983). *American Indians, American Justice*. Austin: University of Texas Press.

Firester, Robert, & Kendall T. Jones (2000). "Catchin' the Heat of the Beat: First Amendment Analysis of Music Claimed to Incite Violence," *Loyola Los Angeles Entertainment Law Journal* 20: 1.

Fried, Carrie B. (1996). "Bad Rap for Rap: Bias in Reactions to Music Lyrics," *Journal of Applied Social Psychology* 26: 2135–2146.

Gallup Organization (2001). "Black-White Relations in the United States 2001 Update," www.gallup.com/poll/speicalReports/pollSummaries/sro10711.

Georges-Abeyie, Daniel (1990). "The Myth of a Racist Criminal Justice System?" In Brian MacLean & Dragan Milovanovic (eds.), *Racism, Empiricism and Criminal Justice*. Vancouver: Collective Press.

Gilfus, Mary E. (1992). "From Victims to Survivors to Offenders: Women's Routes of Entry and Immersion into Street Crime," *Women & Criminal Justice* 4(1): 63–89.

Goldsmith, Andrew E. (2002). "Recent Developments: Criminal Gang Abatement," *Harvard Journal on Legislation* 39: 503.

Gore, Tipper (1987). *Raising PG Kids in an X-Rated World*. Nashville: Abingdon.

Hansen, Christine Hall (1995). "Predicting Cognitive and Behavioral Effects of Gangsta Rap," *Basic and Applied Social Psychology* 16: 43–52.

Harris, David A. (2002). *Profiles in Injustice: Why Racial Profiling Cannot Work.* New York: New Press.

——— (2001). "Addressing Racial Profiling in the States: A Case Study of the 'New Federalism' in Constitutional Criminal Procedure," *University of Pennsylvania Journal of Constitutional Law* 3: 367.

——— (1999). "The Stories, the Statistics and the Law: Why Driving while Black Matters," *Minnesota Law Review* 84(2): 265–326.

Higginbotham, A. Leon, Jr. (1996). *Shades of Freedom: Racial Politics and Presumptions of the American Legal Process.* New York: Oxford University Press.

Higginbotham, E. Michael (2001). *Race Law: Cases, Commentary, and Questions.* Durham, NC: Carolina Academic Press.

Hill, Gary, & Elizabeth M. Crawford (1990). "Women, Race, and Crime," *Criminology* 28(4): 601–623

Holmes, Marvin D. (2000). "Minority Threat and Police Brutality: Determinants of Civil Rights Criminal Complaints in U.S. Municipalities," *Criminology* 38: 343–367.

hooks, bell (1994). *Outlaw Culture: Resisting Representations.* New York: Routledge, 115–123.

——— (1981). *Ain't I a Woman: Black Women and Feminism.* Boston: South End Press.

Johnson, James, Lee Anderson Jackson, & Leslie Gatto (1995). "Violent Attitudes and Deferred Academic Aspirations: Deleterious Effects of Exposure to Rap Music," *Basic and Applied Social Psychology* 16: 27–41.

Johnson, Kevin (2000). "The Case against Race Profiling in Immigration Enforcement," *Washington University Law Quarterly* 78(3): 675–736.

Johnson, Paula (1995). "At the Intersection of Injustice: Experiences of African American Women in Crime and Sentencing" *American University Journal of Gender and the Law* 4: 1–76.

Kennedy, Randall (2002). *Nigger: The Strange Career of a Troublesome Word.* New York: Pantheon.

——— (1999). "Suspect Policy," *The New Republic* 34, September 13 & 20.

Lauritsen, Janet L., & Robert Sampson (1998). "Minorities, Crime, and Justice." In Michael Tonry (ed.) *The Handbook of Crime & Punishment.* New York: Oxford University Press.

Lawrence, Charles, III (1987). "The Id, the Ego, and Equal Protection: Reckoning with Unconscious Racism," *Stanford Law Review* 39: 317.

Lester, D. (1999). *Crime and the Native American.* Springfield, IL: Charles C. Thomas.

Lopez, Ian Haney (2000). "Institutional Racism: Judicial Conduct and a New Theory of Racial Discrimination," *Yale Law Journal* 109: 1717.

Lundman, Richard, & Robert Kaufman (2003). "Driving While Black: Effects of Race, Ethnicity, and Gender on Citizen Self-reports of Traffic Stops and Police Actions," *Criminology* 41(1): 195–220.

Massey, Douglas & Nancy Denton (1993). *American Apartheid* Cambridge, MA: Harvard University Press.

Mastrofski, Stephen, Michael Reisig, & John McCluskey (2002). "Police Disrespect toward the Public: An Encounter-Based Analysis," *Criminology* 40(3): 519.

Mauer, Marc, & Meda Chesney-Lind (eds.) (2002). *Invisible Punishment: The Collateral Consequences of Mass Incarceration.* New York: New Press.

Mauer, Marc, & Tracy Huling (1995). "Young Black Americans and the Criminal Justice System: Five Years Later." Washington, DC, The Sentencing Project.

McCord, Joan, Cathy Spatz Wisdom, & Nancy Crowell (eds.) (2001). *Juvenile Crime, Juvenile Justice.* Washington, DC: National Academies Press, 228–259.

Meeks, Kenneth (2000). *Driving while Black: Highways, Shopping Malls, Taxicabs, Sidewalks: How to Fight Back if You Are a Victim of Racial Profiling.* New York: Broadway Books.

Milovanovic, Dragan, & Katheryn K. Russell (eds.) (2001). *Petit Apartheid in the U.S. Criminal Justice System.* Durham, NC: Carolina Academic Press.

Nelson, Jill (ed.) (2000). *Police Brutality.* New York: W. W. Norton.

Neilsen, Marianne, & Robert A. Silverman (eds.) (1996). *Native Americans, Crime and Justice.* Boulder, CO: Westview Press.

Nunn, Kenneth (2002). "Race, Crime, and the Pool of Surplus Criminality: or Why the 'War on Drugs' Was a 'War on Blacks'" *Gender, Race and Justice* 6: 381.

Ogletree, Charles (2000). "The Role of Race in the U.S. Criminal Justice System and the Opportunities for International Responses." International Human Rights Law Group, U.S. Program, presented to the United Nations Commission on Human Rights, 56th Session, April 5, 2000, Geneva, Switzerland.

Paul-Emile, Kimani (1999). "The Charleston Policy: Substance or Abuse?" *Michigan Journal of Race and the Law* 4: 325.

Peterson, Ruth, & John Hagan (1984). "Changing Conceptions of Race: Towards an Account of Anomalous Findings of Sentencing Research," *American Sociological Review* 49 (February): 56–70.

Ritchie, Beth (1996). *Compelled to Crime: The Gender Entrapment of Battered Black Women.* New York: Routledge.

Ross, Luana (1998). *Inventing the Savage: The Social Construction of Native American Criminality.* Austin: University of Texas Press.

Russell, Katheryn K. (1999). "'Driving while Black': Corollary Phenomena and Collateral Consequences," *Boston College Law Review* 40(3): 717–731.
—— (1998). *The Color of Crime: Racial Hoaxes, White Fear, Black Protectionism, Police Harassment and Other Macroaggressions.* New York: New York University Press.
Sampson, Robert, & Janet Lauritsen (1997). "Racial and Ethnic Disparities in Crime and Criminal Justice in the United States." In Michael Tonry (ed.), *Ethnicity, Crime and Immigration: Comparative and Cross-National Perspectives.* Chicago: University of Chicago Press, 311–374.
Siedschlaw, Kurt, & James N. Gilbert (1994). "Native Americans in Criminal Justice." In J. Hendricks & B. Byers (eds.), *Multicultural Perspectives in Criminal Justice and Criminology.* Springfield, IL: Charles C. Thomas, 135–153.
Silliman, Jael, & Anannya Bhattacharjee (eds.) (2002). *Policing the National Body: Race, Gender and Criminalization.* Boston: South End Press.
Simpson, Sally S. (1989). "Feminist Theory, Crime, and Justice," *Criminology* 27: 605–631.
Spohn, Cassia (2000). "Thirty Years of Sentencing Reform: The Quest for a Racially Neutral Sentencing Process." *Policies, Processes and Decisions of the Criminal Justice Process.* Washington, DC: National Institute of Justice.
Sudbury, Julia (2002). "Celling Black Bodies: Black Women in the Global Prison Industrial Complex," *Feminist Review* 70: 57–74.
Tatum, Becky L. (1999). "The Link between Rap Music and Youth Crime and Violence: A Review of the Literature and Issues for Future Research," *The Justice Professional* 11: 353–359.
Tonry, Michael, & Joan Petersilia (eds.) (1999). *Prisons.* Chicago: University of Chicago Press.
Turner, Patricia (1993). *I Heard It through the Grapevine: Rumor in African-American Culture.* Berkeley: University of California Press.
U.S. Department of Justice (2003). "Prevalence of Imprisonment in the U.S. Population, 1974–2001," NCJ 197976. Washington, DC.
—— (2002). "Crime in the United States, 2001: Uniform Crime Reports." Washington, DC.
—— (2002). "Hispanic Victims of Violent Crime, 1993–2000." NCJ 191208. Washington, DC
—— (2002). "Prisoners in 2001." NCJ 195189. Washington, DC.
—— (2002). "Federal Cocaine Offenses: An Analysis of Crack and Powder Penalties." Washington, DC.
—— (2002). "Probation and Parole in the United States." NCJ 195669. Washington, DC.
—— (2002). "Criminal Victimization 2001." NCJ 194610. Washington, DC.

——— (2002). "Recidivism of Prisoners Released in 1994." NCJ 193427. Washington, DC.

——— (2001). "Contacts between Police and the Public: Findings from the 1999 National Survey." NCJ 184957. Washington, DC.

——— (2001). "Policing and Homicide, 1976–1998: Justifiable Homicide by Police, Police Officers Murdered by Felons." NCJ-180987. Washington, DC.

——— (1997). "Lifetime Likelihood of Going to State or Federal Prison." NCJ-160092. Washington, DC.

Weisburd, David, Stanton Wheeler, Elin Waring, & Nancy Bode (1991). *Crime of the Middle Classes: White-Collar Offenders in the Federal Courts.* New Haven: Yale University Press.

Weitzer, Ronald (2000). "Racialized Policing: Residents' Perceptions in Three Neighborhoods," *Law and Society Review* 34: 129–155.

Weitzer, Ronald, & Steven Tuch (2002). "Perceptions of Racial Profiling: Race, Class, and Personal Experience," *Criminology* 40(2): 435.

Williams, Patricia J. (1997). *Seeing a Color-Blind Future: The Paradox of Race.* New York: Noonday.

Young, Vernetta (1990). "Women, Race & Crime," *Criminology* 18(1): 26–34.

Zatz, Marjorie (1987). "The Changing Forms of Racial/Ethnic Biases in Sentencing," *Journal of Research on Crime and Delinquency* 24: 69.

Index

abortion and crime rates, 111–113, 117
affirmative action, 56–57, 119
African Americans. *See* Blacks
Alexie, Sherman, 24
American Indian College Fund, 24–25
American Indians, 20–34; applicable legal systems 29–30; arrests of, 138; Civil Rights Act and, 26–27; criminal justice system and, 20–21, 29–33; death row and, 142; definition of, 21–22; federal laws and, 29–30; Justice Department report on, 30–31; population statistics, 23, 33; public images of, 23–29; racial labels, 21–22; 23; racial profiling of, n.157; use of names for sports teams, 26–29; victimization rates, 31–32, 137
Arab Americans, and racial profiling, 100
Arnold, Regina, 131
Asian Americans: control rates, 128,136, 138; death row and, 141–142; population, 32; victimization, 137
Assimilative Crimes Act, 29
Atlanta Braves, 26, 27–28
Austin, Regina, 75–76, 92

Bain, Bryonn, 108
Ballard, Mary, 47–48
Barongan, Christy, 45, 151 n.28
Barry, Marion, 80, 81, 82–83, 87, 89–90, 93
Bauer, Eddie, 109
Bennett, William, 42,
Bertrand, Marianne, 160 n.38
Binder, Amy, 51, 53
Black, Donald, 12, 13
Black protectionism, 72–96

Blacks: arrests, *generally*, 97, 118, 138; control rates, 136, 138, 140, 141; death row, 141–142; drug-related crime, 140; federal offenses, 140; opinions on, 100; perceptions of the justice, 77; recidivism rates and, 137; victimization rates, 137,138; white-collar crime, 139
Black women: control rates, 122–126; 136, 161 n.10; crack cocaine use, 139; offending by, 127–128; drug crime and, 127; justice system and, 119–134; racial profiling of, 17,132–133; recidivism rates, 137; research on, 130–133; stereotypes of, 119; victimization of, 128, 129; 130
Brooke, Edward, 81
Bureau of Indian Affairs, 22
Busch, Gidone, 58
Bush, George H. W., 88
Bush, George W., 43, 82, 97
Butler, Paul, 108
Butts, Calvin, 42
Bryant, Kobe, 40
Bynum, Tim, 10

Carrington, Kerry, 162 n.36
Carruth, Rae, 80, 81, 91
Charleston v. Ferguson, 17, 114
Chavez v. Illinois, p. 102, 103, 104
Chicago v. Morales, 14–15, 108
Clinton, Bill, 81, 84, 85, 86, 87, 93, 94, 95, 97, 116, 156 n.34
Coates, Steven, 47–48
cocaine; crack use by race, 139; federal crack law, 128, 139; fetal endangerment laws and, 17

About the Author

KATHERYN RUSSELL-BROWN is Professor of Law and Director of the Center for the Study of Race and Race Relations at the University of Florida's Law School. She taught criminology at the University of Maryland for eleven years and has also taught at the American University Law School, City University of New York (CUNY) Law School, Howard, and Alabama State University. Professor Russell-Brown received her undergraduate degree from the University of California, Berkeley, her law degree from the University of California, Hastings, and her Ph.D. from the University of Maryland. Dr. Russell-Brown's 1994 article "The Constitutionality of Jury Override in Alabama Death Penalty Cases," was cited by the U.S. Supreme Court in *Harris v. Alabama* (1995). Her first book, *The Color of Crime: Racial Hoaxes, White Fear, Black Protectionism, Police Harassment, and Other Macroaggressions,* was published in 1998 by NYU Press.

Please send any questions or comments to her e-mail address: undergroundcodes@law.ufl.edu.